Discipleship According to Jesus
"A Definitive Look at Discipleship"

Fred Campbell

TOWNSEND**PRESS**

Copyright © 2019 by Fred Campbell

Scripture quotations marked KJV are from the King James Version of the Bible.

Those marked NKJV are taken from the New King James Version®. Copyright © 1982 by Thomas Nelson. Used by permission. All rights reserved.

Those marked NIV are from the Holy Bible, NEW INTERNATIONAL VERSION® Copyright © 1973, 1978, 1984, 2011 by Biblica, Inc. ® Used by permission. All rights reserved worldwide.

Those marked NASB are from the New American Standard Bible®. Copyright © 1960, 1962, 1963, 1968, 1971, 1972, 1973, 1975, 1977, 1995 by The Lockman Foundation. Used by permission. (www.Lockman.org)

Scripture quotations marked (ESV) are taken from the Holy Bible, English Standard Version® (ESV®), copyright © 2001 by Crossway, a publishing ministry of Good News Publishers. Used by permission. All rights reserved.

Scripture quotations marked ASV are taken from the American Standard Version of the Bible.

All rights reserved. No part of this book may be reproduced or transmitted in any form, by any means, electronic or mechanical, including photocopying, recording, or by any information storage or retrieval system without the expressed permission in writing from the publisher. Permission requests may be addressed to Townsend Press, P. O. Box 70990, Nashville, Tennessee 37207-0990; or e-mailed to customercare@sspbnbc.com.

Printed and bound in the United States of America

ISBN: 978-1-949052-12-1

*In memory of Joyce Elane,
my Beloved Wife of forty-nine years who,
on June 13, 2011,
left me for a better Man and
went upstairs to live eternally with Him.*

*And to the wonderful Children of this union:
Fred Kevin Campbell
Teresa Lynn Campbell Pleasant
Yvette Elaine Campbell
Sean Duane Campbell
Anthony Troy Campbell
Kyla Juliet Campbell*

TABLE OF CONTENTS

Foreword vii

Acknowledgments x

Introduction 1

The First Thought: *The Obedient Church* 4
    Partial Obedience Is Disobedience 6
    Obedience: A Characteristic of the People of God 7
    Sounds of Disobedience 8
    Negligent Disobedience 9

The Second Thought: *Beyond the Meaning to Jesus' Model of Making a Disciple* 20
    Members of the Multitude 22
    An Obedient Follower 24
    Beyond Belief 25
    Jesus Is Lord 29
    A Closer Look at Matthew 28:18-20 32
    The Missional Church under Mandate 33
    The Preaching Church 35

The Third Thought: *Making Disciples through Relationships* 38
    Christ Is Relational 40
    The Men 40
    God with Us 41
    Body Life 42
    The Body of Christ's Social Response to the World 44
    The Indicative Perspective 46
    Relational Discipleship 48
    The Family and Relational Discipleship 49
    The Pastoral Family Paradigm 50

    Discipleship in the Marriage 51
    The Christian Family... 52
    The Wife as a Disciple Maker 54
    The Foundation 55

The Fourth Thought: *Making Disciples through Reflection* 63
    The General Revelation of God... 63
    Image Bearers.. 65
    Marred Image... 66
    Conformed to Christ's Image 72
    The Revelation of God...76
    Reflection 80
    Transformation Is in Continuum 86

The Fifth Thought: *Reproducing Disciples*... 91
    Jesus' Analogy of Reproduction (John 15).. 92
    Multiplication: The Most Effective Method of Church Growth 94
    Discipleship and Social Justice 98
    Church and Discipleship 101

The Final Thought: *Residential Presence in the Disciple* 105

The Afterthought: *Discipleship According to Jesus* 110
    The First Person 114
    The Significance of Coming to Him.. 114
    The Significance of Our New Relationship..116
    The Significance of Prioritizing 117
    The Significance of the Cross in the Life of Disciples................................118
    The Significance of Complete Christianity... 121

The Final Afterthought: *This Is Discipleship According to Jesus* 124

Bibliography 125

FOREWORD

Making disciples is certainly a significant part of what churches are commanded to do. Through *proclamation*, we are to initiate the unbeliever into the faith. Through *spiritual therapy* we are to inspire the mature believer to keep the faith. Through *discipleship* we are to instruct the new believer about the faith so that he or she grows in spiritual maturity—no longer living in the realm of spiritual infancy and drinking milk but, rather, flourishing in the precincts of spiritual maturity, eating meat, and making disciples. This is what Dr. Fred Campbell seeks to teach in his book *Discipleship According to Jesus*. And he chooses to do it according to the way Jesus did it—by admonishing readers to make disciples and not just to seek to add members.

Dr. Campbell posits that discipleship according to Jesus must be personal and steeped with obedience as exemplified by Jesus' method in Mark 3:13-15 (ESV): "*And he went up on the mountain and c*alled to him those whom he desired, and they came to him. *And he appointed twelve (whom he also named apostles) so that they might be with him and he might s*end them out to preach and have authority to cast out demons" (emphasis added). Jesus spent time developing His disciples and consequently could expect their obedience when He sent them out. In this work, Dr. Campbell shines a bright light into the dark places under which many have church—we can call ourselves an Evangelism Church, Christian Education Church, Praise and Worship Church, Social Justice Church, Christian Leadership Church, or any of many other names we could choose. However, if we are not obeying Jesus' last words as the foundation for our activity, then we are, as Dr. Campbell posits, a Disobedient Church.

For Fred Campbell, evangelism without discipleship is truncation—it does not go far enough in developing new believers into mature soldiers in God's army. Dr. Campbell's method is Jesus' method—it is discipleship through sanctification, or as Paul puts it in Colossians 1:28, *"that we may present everyone mature in Christ"* (ESV). There are new models and glitzy methods of discipleship that are appealing and attractive, but Campbell argues in this work that our eyes must be on Jesus and our hearts imbued with the Great Commission, Jesus' Last Will and Testament.

Dr. Fred Campbell diagnoses the problem with today's church model and copies the prescription Jesus gave to His Body—go and make disciples. He has the penchant to state the truth of Scripture in fresh, new ways without compromising the truths of Scripture. He does this without yielding to clichés and short-lasting verbal novelties. In fact, Dr. Campbell unabashedly and clearly advocates for the cause of Christ and the mission of the biblically obedient church. He waves a broad spotlight and a pointed stick as he overturns our calm tables of doing church as usual.

I know many churches that are busy—busy running revivals, busy tweeting, busy posting on Instagram or Facebook, busy crafting pithy, short, and memorable statements, busy trying to acquire the next church gadget, busy chasing the next big Minister of Music, busy trying to secure a great YouTube following, busy with text blasts, busy making sure the right cars are in the parking lot, busy making sure the right people are greeted and seated, busy making sure family pictures are perfect, and busy saying the right things. These churches are busy doing the work of the Lord, but are they too busy to really obey the Lord? Jesus charged His church to make disciples who can make disciples. Dr. Campbell exposes the busyness of the Body of Christ that deviates from Jesus' model of discipleship and is a way that seems right, but the end thereof leads to perpetual spiritual immaturity. In Luke 10:25-28, the rich young ruler asked Jesus what he must do to inherit eternal life. Jesus asked him about his understanding of Scripture. The young ruler answered correctly and Jesus told him to obey what he understood. I encourage you to study the pages of *Discipleship According to Jesus* from my friend, brother, and watchman on the tower. In these pages, Dr. Fred Campbell helps you understand the Scriptures regarding discipleship, issues a clarion call to return to biblical discipleship—a call our culture desperately needs as we prepare for the second coming of our Lord—and invites you to obey what you have understood.

Dr. Robert Smith Jr.
Charles T. Carter Baptist Chair of Divinity
Beeson Divinity School
Samford University

ACKNOWLEDGMENTS

I am indebted to Doris Williams and Alisha Harris for their invaluable assistance in the completion of this work.

I am also grateful to the Mount Zion Baptist Church, Redwood City, California, who has afforded me the freedom to research and write this discipline on *Discipleship According to Jesus.*

The people of this congregation have made a profound investment into the growth of this author and pastor for more than forty years. I am better because of them.

Thank God for these six men of God who have helped me think critically, carefully, and biblically about the subject of Discipleship.

Dr. Robert Smith Jr.
Charles T. Carter Baptist Chair of Divinity
Beeson School of Divinity at Samford University in Birmingham, Alabama

Ervin Carl Wilson, pastor
Community Church, East Palo Alto, California

Albert Johnson, pastor
New Genesis Church, Austell, Georgia

Welton Pleasant II, pastor
Christ Second Baptist Church, Long Beach, California

Maurice M. Harris Sr.
Graduate of Gateway Seminary, Ontario, California

Dr. Jerry Young, pastor and president
New Hope Baptist Church, Jackson, Mississippi, and the National Baptist Convention, USA, Inc.

INTRODUCTION

"The Last Must Not Become the Least"

The unhealthiness and ineffectiveness of today's church can be attributed to the church's failure to obey the last thing that Jesus said for her to do. Last things are often important things to consider. The last will and testament is more important than the first. It is definitive in nature and character. It normally carries more weight than that which preceded it. Last words are often thoughtful words. They are words that have gone through the crucibles of life. They are not words of the immature but of the sages and seers. They are not normally anxious words but urgent words. They are not emotive words, but evolving words. Last words often demand hearing and heeding. We dare not trifle with them. Words uttered at the end of life are more powerful than words uttered at the beginning of life. Last words are often benedictory and missional in nature. They bless and beckon us to go.

Now may the God of peace who brought again from the dead our Lord Jesus, the great shepherd of the sheep, by the blood of the eternal covenant, equip you with everything good that you may do his will, working in us that which is pleasing in his sight, through Jesus Christ, to whom be glory forever and ever. Amen.[1]

They are "now and therefore" words serving as conjunctions. Last words command and commission us to engage in ministry.

"A new commandment I give to you, that you love one another: just as I have loved you, you also are to love one another. By this all people will know that you are my disciples, if you have love for one another."[2]

"Go therefore and make disciples of all nations, baptizing them in the name of the Father and of the Son and of the Holy Spirit, teaching them to observe all

---

1. The Holy Bible: Hebrews 13:20-21 (ESV)
2. The Holy Bible: John 13:34-35 (ESV)

that I have commanded you. And behold, I am with you always, to the end of the age."[3]

The last words of Jesus, who is the Living Word and centerpiece or personality of all of Scripture, need to be heeded. The valedictory statement of Jesus quoted above found in what we call the "Great Commission" calls for an obedient response from His Church. It is a command—not a suggestion—to make disciples as we go into our world and the world. It is not the only thing He said in His closing days on earth, and perhaps not the very last thing He said, but the clarion call in the *Great Commission* with Trinitarian authority gives credence to its being the last thing of which we must not make the least thing we do as Christians and the Church.

Therefore, since the final act of our salvation has been achieved through the incarnation, atonement, and resurrection of this Jesus, Son of Man and Son of God, the first disciples of Jesus had their talking points and waited only for the necessary power (Acts 1:8) to accomplish Christ's global vision of making disciples of all nations. It is Jesus and His first disciples who model for us the what, the why, the when, and the wherefore of discipleship. Our observation of Jesus' unique relationship with these twelve men, including Judas, is invaluable to understanding what it means to be a disciple who makes disciples of Christ. The early believers were called disciples. They were not even known as Christians (Acts 11:26). They were known as Jesus' disciples. His disciples did not choose the term "Christian." It was an anti-Christian sentiment. As we explore this topic, we will see the significance of this reality.

It is my desire that in reading this discipline you will rediscover that the "last thing Jesus said," in the words of Robby Gallaty, must become "our first work."[4] The focus of this book is to get the Christian and the Church to obey that last thing Jesus told His Church to engage in. It must not become optional. It must not become dispensational—thus, a

---

3. The Holy Bible: Matthew 28:19-20 (ESV)

4. Robby Gallaty, *Rediscovering Discipleship: Making Jesus' Final Words Our First Work* (Grand Rapids, Michigan: Zondervan, 2015), 16.

past function of the Church of Jesus Christ. It is significantly called the *Great Commission,* for it is the timeless strategy of Christ, the Head of His Church. His greatness makes the command to make disciples too great for us to ignore and relegate it to the thing we engage in the least. To do less in His Church is a sin. To make disciple making a ministry and not the ministry of His Church is to cease being the Church of Christ.

The First Thought: The Obedient Church

What kind of Church is your Church?

Jesus informed His disciples in response to Peter's revelation that He would build His Church upon Himself and upon those who possessed His nature (Matthew 16:18). Our churches are not necessarily His Church. There are all kinds of churches inside of Christianity. There are churches with various denominational distinctions. There are churches that pride themselves on having no denominational distinctions. There are churches that separate themselves as conservative, liberal, charismatic, non-charismatic, Pentecostal, holiness, confirming, universal, orthodox, reform, and so forth. There are churches that are known for their music, social emphasis, mission endeavors, evangelistic fervor, preaching prowess, and ethnicity. Let me be bold enough here and say without equivocation that His Church is an Obedient Church.

There can be diversity at this point. According to how one interprets Scripture, churches can become different kinds of churches. Churches can emphasize different kinds of focuses and objectives. For instance, in Jesus' inaugural address found in Luke 4, you can make room for a social-justice kind of church. In Matthew 25:35-46, we can make room for a mission-benevolent kind of church. The parable of the Good Samaritan pleads for a good-neighbor kind of church (Luke 10:25-47). The Great Commandment passage (see John 13:34-35) cries out for a loving kind of church. While I may argue with the resultant interpretation of some of the passages aforementioned, I shall not argue with the validity of the passages. But I will say that they must bow to the last thing that Jesus said to His disciples. They must not be an end, but a means to the end of making disciples.

The church in North America is said to be on the decline, dying and headed for extinction. The majority of the members are older and their children are unimpressed and uncommitted to the church of their forbearers. Is the decline a matter of disobedience or our obedience? I believe that it is a matter of both disobedience and obedience. The desertion experienced in the church can be of an apostate nature. Members are leaving perhaps because they were not born and baptized into the church (1 John 2:29). I will explain that point later in the book. The church may be declining to its authentic reality. The apostle Paul warned Timothy, his timid son in the ministry, *"that in later times some will depart from the faith."*[5] The departure from the church may be caused by the fact that they have not obeyed the Gospel (Romans 10:16). We must not fully be alarmed at the exodus from the church. Declaring the cost of discipleship can hinder the numerical growth of the church and be the reason for the decline in the church (John 6:64-71). Being an obedient church does not guarantee church growth, but it does enable church health.

Fans of Christ are attracted to a gospel of accommodation instead of the Gospel of the cross. Apostle Paul called them members with "itching ears."[6] Today, they are children of this pluralistic, post-modern subjective truth age and are not authentic followers of Christ. They are the product of cheap grace and easy beliefism. They may have come to church, but not to Christ—there is a difference. Fandom members have surface faith. It is faith that believes only in the existence of God, but does not rest in the finished work of Christ. That type of faith will not endure the storms that come from following Jesus. An obedient church is better able to lead

---

5. The Holy Bible: 1 Timothy 4:1 (ESV)
6. The Holy Bible: 2 Timothy 4:3 (ESV)

members of the fandom crowd to authentically follow Christ. (I will speak more on this later in the book.) Even though they are more apt to desert the church, not all fans abandon the church. They do, however, often transfer to accommodating churches, or churches that, to them, appear to be accommodating. When churches grow due to members' transferring their membership, this is called "transfer growth," which is not the best growth, because it is not new growth. And although the church is seen as growing, it is not necessarily healthy.

Some churches are experiencing phenomenal growth due to members' transferring from one church to another, but these churches are just filling up with fans. This is not to say that everyone who comes to your church from another church is a fan. But those who do transfer need discipleship vetting to keep your church from becoming unhealthy. A letter of transfer is helpful, but a discipleship process is much better. A fan-filled church can become a church filled with authentic followers of Christ, especially in a disciple-making church. Disciple-making churches are healthy churches because the members (aka, the "sheep") are being fed a healthy diet of what it takes to be a disciple of Christ. A great indicator of whether or not the members are being fed is their spiritual weight. Are the sheep emaciated or are they healthy? Are they living and thriving, or they starving and dying? It would do the shepherd well to be less concerned with counting the sheep and more concerned with weighing them. Numerical growth of a church is not necessarily indicative of a healthy church.

Partial Obedience Is Disobedience

The *Great Commission* is Jesus' command for His church to embrace His global vision and ultimate strategy for reaching the entire world with the Gospel of grace. The command in the verb form—*make disciples*—is given by Jesus, who has the authority by virtue of His Lordship and saving activity. The church, Christ's mystical presence on earth, was commanded, as each member of His Body engages their world to make disciples. They are called to live out a life of making disciples where they work, live, learn, and play. He who purchased the church by His blood (Acts 20:28), owner and head, calls for obedience. A church that will fully embrace and obey the last thing He said for His church to do—*go make disciples*—is the *kind* of church He desires and designed: an obedient church—nothing more, nothing less. Obedience characterizes the people and church of God. The mother of the Israelites obeyed Abraham, the father of the Israelites: *"Sarah obeyed Abraham, calling him lord. And you are her children, if you do good and do not fear anything that is frightening."*[7] The apostle Paul also admonished, *"Wives, submit to your own husbands, as to the Lord. For the husband is the head of the wife even as Christ is the head of the church, his body, and is himself its Savior."*[8]

Sarah represented the people of God, and Christian wives represented the church of Christ. Both were ordered to obey and submit to authority. These two examples cause great consternation for women in general and wives in particular. But the purposeful God is drawing a bigger picture through the obedience and submission of wives. *(I hope the opposite is true, but at this point in my writing, I'm afraid that I may have lost the interest of most of my female readers, especially those who have experienced abuse because of the misunderstanding of male headship. I urge you to read on.)* The purpose of God, which is to demonstrate how an obedient wife exemplifies an obedient people and church, cannot be altered because man has chosen to misuse and misinterpret the Scripture to objectify and devalue women.

Obedience: A Characteristic of the People of God

Israel came out of Abraham's loins and was set apart from all other nations to be an obedient people. Their distinction was not primarily nationalistic in nature but more missional, and that mission was to accomplish God's great plan for the entire world. As a people, they were

---

7. The Holy Bible: 1 Peter 3:6 (ESV)
8. The Holy Bible: Ephesians 5:22-23 (ESV)

blessed to be a blessing (Genesis 12:1-3). When they were disobedient, they contradicted their missional purpose. Abraham, the father of faith, modeled obedience; but, at times, he was disobedient, which resulted in costly lessons learned. Abraham was not only a consequential figure of human history—fathering two nations—but he was also the father of all those who believe [Romans 4:1-25].

Sounds of Disobedience

Saul was the first king of Israel and was a miserable failure because he thought that partial obedience would satisfy the LORD if it was cloaked in rituals and religious performances. As king, he experienced some measure of success while being partially disobedient (which is dangerous), but he soon found out that incomplete obedience was the equivalent of complete disobedience. Saul and the people of Israel did not fully obey the words of the LORD. Saul substituted the will of God with the will of the people of Israel. And, he personally wanted the praise of the people for himself, so he erected a monument in his honor instead of honoring God in obedience. Saul and the people erroneously thought that praise was more important to God than obedience. Church members that are busy *having* church instead of *being* the church possess an equivalent false mindset that God desires burnt offerings and sacrifices more than obedience. Often, under the guise of praising God, congregants are actually focusing on themselves rather than on Him, and in the midst of this false, self-serving worship are the deafening sounds of disobedience.

Unfortunately, the sounds of disobedience can be drowned out by several factors and factions occurring in our churches today, including numerical growth, fiscal solvency, emotionalism, excitement, social involvement, self-serving preaching, evangelistic endeavor, educational efforts, missions and outreach focuses, contemporary and traditional worship, and state-of-the-art buildings. The words of the prophet Samuel were relevant in his day and are still just as relevant today: *"Has the LORD as great delight in burnt offerings and sacrifices, as in obeying the voice of the* LORD*? Behold, to obey is better than sacrifices, and to listen than the fat of rams."*[9] The bleating of the sheep and lowing of the oxen (verse 14) were sounds of disobedience.

Negligent Disobedience

The prophet Jonah was given a direct command by God to go to Nineveh and preach to the people there. Jonah did not want to go, so he went in a different direction and ran from the will and word of God. This was blatant disobedience on Jonah's part. Negligent disobedience, on the other hand, is failing to take proper care in doing what God has commanded. In other words, it means falling short of carrying out God's purpose and plan. It is minoring in what Jesus majored in, and majoring in what Jesus minored in. It is like a hospital administration placing more emphasis on the gift shop and cafeteria than on the purpose of healing. The purpose and plan of the church is to major in what Jesus majored in. The primary purpose of this book is to convey to the reader exactly what Jesus majored in: disciple making. Disciple making is a ministry for everyone (the church), and not just a ministry in the church. In his book *Rediscovering Discipleship,* Robby Gallaty aptly stated that "until disciple-making becomes the ministry of the church and not a ministry in the church, we will never see our discipleship efforts impact the world the way that Jesus envisioned."[10]

Negligent disobedience is often the result of misinterpreting the words, deeds, and purpose of Jesus. For instance, churches that major in healing ministries are practicing something that ended with the apostolic age. They do so simply because they do not interpret miracles as signs of those who had initial authority (see John 3:2; Acts 5:12; 2 Corinthians 12:12). Miracles were primarily performed by Jesus and the apostles in order to authenticate that they were sent from God.

---

9. The Holy Bible: 1 Samuel 15:22 (ESV)
10. Robby Gallaty, *Rediscovering Discipleship* (Grand Rapids, Michigan: Zondervan, 2015), 17.

In name but not in purpose. A disobedient church is a church in name only and not in purpose. When the church functions in disobedience, she is not the church of Jesus Christ, as she is acting inconsistently with Christ, who is the Head of the church. When the actions of the body are inconsistent with the head, stroke-like symptoms are manifested, resulting in dysfunction. This does not mean that the head has been separated from the body, and thanks be to God that the church will never be organically separate from its head; therefore, those who speak of a churchless Christianity are ignorant of the profound nature of the union between the head and the body.

The last thing ought not to become the least thing. The Great Commission was Jesus Christ's last commandment to the church to make disciples, but it must not become the least thing that His church engages in. From my observation, the church has neglected the fulfillment of the command by not fully obeying it because we have misunderstood the strategy for reaching the world with the Gospel of grace and, therefore, the church suffers and the world goes un-reached. The disobedient church has become sick, unhealthy, and, subsequently, ineffective in making, marking, maturing, and multiplying disciples. In short, a sick church cannot reach a sick world and falls short in fulfilling the mandate of the Master.

Missions. A church that is missional without intentional discipleship is negligibly disobedient. The making of a disciple ought to be the end product of our mission thrust. To reach the world with the love of Jesus Christ is not complete without the goal of making, marking, maturing, and multiplying disciples. If there is no focus on making disciples, then our mission effects are no more than what the Red Cross and other caring agencies do. If we are the church of Jesus Christ, then discipleship must be intentional. The mission of the church is to send disciples into the world to make disciples of all nations. "There is not something called Christianity and then missionaries who spread it. Christianity is in its very essence a mission to the world. If it is not reaching, teaching, baptizing, and multiplying disciples, it is not Christianity."[11]

Our mission to the world is not to be loved by the world—although, in love, we go into the world. But because the true nature of the Gospel is ambiguous (Mark 16:15-16), we go into the world with both good and bad news (Romans 6:23) and are subject to being rejected and ridiculed (2 Timothy 1:8-12). If the endeavor of mission work is merely to care for the material and physical needs of people, then why is this faced with suffering and persecution? The reality of mission work is that the ultimate purpose of the church mission is to go out into the world to make disciples and this conflicts with the world—thus the persecution and suffering. The church is more than the Red Cross; it is a community of cross-bearing disciples who are not ashamed of the Gospel of grace, for it has the power to transform lives (Romans 1:16).

The world and Jesus' disciples attempted to deter Him to get Him off His mission for the sake of political, social, and nationalistic needs and desires, but in His suffering, He exemplified obedience to His mission which was culminated on a hill called Calvary, where He paid the price for human redemption. Therefore, the Father sent Him into the world as He sends His Church into the world with the ministry and message of reconciliation (John 17:18; 2 Corinthians 5:17-21).

Social Justice. Striving for social justice in the midst of injustice honors those who suffered so much to bring us the social freedom that we now benefit from; but, we do not honor Christ if discipleship is not the intentional goal of social liberation. We must not seek to gain our rights without seeking to be right with God, which is the intent of comprehensive discipleship. Through social justice, we gain our equality from unjust tyrants and systematic racism, but through comprehensive discipleship, we gain ultimate freedom from tyrannies of Satan, the flesh, and a fallen world

---
11. Michael Horton, *The Gospel Commission* (Grand Rapids, Michigan: Baker Books, 2011), 87.

system. Social freedom without spiritual freedom is really no freedom at all. It is only supposed freedom. A social gospel is no gospel without spiritual liberation. It is like finding fool's gold. True freedom belongs to those whom the Son sets free (John 8:31-38). Obedience to him who is the truth (John 14:6) is the consummate freedom that humanity truly needs. I believe Jesus' manifesto found in Luke 4:14-30 has more to do with the spiritual than the social; any social benefits that may occur stem from the spiritual. The Jews in the Luke 4:14-30 passage felt that their national connection with Abraham rendered them free. They believed that God was on their side because of who they were ethnically. But Jesus told them that true freedom was only found in relationship with Him. Races of people who take pride in their ethnicity need to humble themselves to the fact that in Christ alone lies true freedom and worth.

There is Divine concern for social injustice. It is disobedient for the church to ignore injustice and human suffering. It was so in Amos's day (Amos 5:18-24) as well as in these times. Concern for the needy and marginalized must be the response of the people of God and the Church of God. But it must be driven by the admonishment of Jesus: *"For what will it profit a man if he gains the whole world and forfeits his soul?"* [12] In our quest for social justice, we must be cognizant that God requires justice. We want social justice, and God demands justice in relation to His holiness. This truth says that the human race has a greater need: to obey the Great Commission, which is Christ's strategy for meeting that greater need. Under God's justice, we are in need of God's grace. Social justice is a cry for fairness; but fairness does not take precedence when we stand before a righteous and holy God. If the church focuses on social justice and neglects pronouncing man's greater need for the righteousness of Christ (Romans 5:18-21; 2 Corinthians 5:17-21), the church may become deaf to the bleating of the sheep and lowing of the oxen and become negligent to the command of Christ to make disciples.

---

12. The Holy Bible: Matthew 16:26a (ESV)

Evangelism. The Great Commission is about winning the lost through the strategy of making disciples. The sounds of disobedience can be drowned out by evangelism that is not contextualized in making disciples. When new growth is not borne out of discipleship in the evangelistic church, that church is guilty of negligent disobedience, or partial obedience. The negligently disobedient evangelistic church focuses on addition, while an obedient disciple-making church is more concerned with multiplication. The health of the body of Christ is enabled by growth through multiplication rather than addition. Jim Wallis rightly said that "the great tragedy of modern evangelism is in calling many to belief but few to obedience. The failure has come in separating belief from obedience, which renders the gospel message confusing and strips the evangelistic proclamation of its power and authority."[13]

He further stated, "In fact, a clear proclamation of the gospel with the demonstrated power to 'make disciples' is precisely what is most lacking in the churches."[14] Then he said, "The call to faith and to discipleship is the same and cannot be separated."[15]

Evangelism contextualized in making disciples prevents a cheap grace response to the Gospel. Some believe discipleship to be second-semester Christianity. Therefore, there are no demands in initial salvation. Easy believism is the misconception that salvation comes without the need to deny self and take up the cross. This is faith without obedience, which is not biblical faith. I will say more about this later. If mere belief was enough for salvation, then the rich young ruler was mistreated (Matthew 19:16-30). Jim Wallis made another observation when he wrote, "It is seldom asked how many have been turned away because of the radical claims Christ is making on their lives. A dangerous respect for numerical success had led to reducing the demands of the gospel, blurring the meaning of discipleship, and accommodating the evangelistic message to what the audience will find

---

13. Jim Wallis, *Agenda for Biblical People* (New York: Harper & Row Publishers, 1976), 23.
14. Ibid.
15. Ibid., 26.

more easily acceptable."[16] I reiterate that the decline in church attendance may be the result of the high demands of the Gospel. The Gospel is *"the power of God unto salvation."*[17] When Christ saves us, He does something for us and radically within us.

Disciple making involves radical change, and real belief is inseparable from the new birth. Becoming a Christian involves more than making a decision for Christ. It involves a dynamic, life-changing experience (John 3:3; Romans 6:4; 2 Corinthians 5:17). John MacArthur said it best when he wrote, "The mission of the church and the goal of evangelism are to make disciples."[18] There are some who would suggest that belief with demands equates to salvation through works. It is unfathomable to think that a person can truly believe and become a Christian and yet not follow and obey Christ. But nominal Christians do not obey Christ's demand to make disciples. Therefore, it is possible to be a Christian and not follow and obey Christ. Nominal Christianity evolves from the notion that a person can be a Christian without being a disciple of Christ. Jesus placed demands on Nicodemus (John 3). He would not enter into the kingdom without the new birth experience. Jesus told the fans (the crowd) that before they could authentically follow Him, they had to first come to Him (Luke 14:26, 27). To come to Him is to bow at His feet in faith and submit to His Lordship (Romans 10:9).

The evangel is best presented and shared in the process of making a disciple. Disciples make disciples. As previously mentioned, discipleship is growth through multiplication, and evangelistic church growth comes by way of addition. The last instruction from the Lord to His motley crew was to make disciples—not to evangelize. Evangelism through disciple making results in a healthy church.

---

16. Ibid., 28.
17. The Holy Bible: Romans 1:16 (KJV)
18. John MacArthur Jr., *The Gospel According to Jesus* (Grand Rapids, Michigan: Zondervan Publishing House, 1988), 221.

Christian Education. Christian education that is not concerned with maturing disciples into the image of Christ is engaged in negligent disobedience. Teachers must see themselves as disciple makers. Christians are to be transformed by the renewing of the mind (Romans 12:1-2). Cognition is part of the process. But the ultimate goal is incarnational growth. The preacher and teacher must become so pregnant with the truth of Scripture that they suffer with labor pains until Christ is formed in the hearer (Galatians 4:19). The truth handlers are responsible for conveying the mind of Christ to the minds of the hearers. This is done with the aid of the Spirit of truth in the Word of truth primarily concerning Jesus who is the truth. The purpose of preaching and teaching truth is to equip the hearer to tell the truth about Jesus the truth. The disciple of Christ as a witness is an ontological truth teller (Acts 1:8). Those who handle the Word of God must rightly divide the truth of Scripture (2 Timothy 2:15). They must cut it straight and walk it straight. They must proclaim and demonstrate the truth of Scripture in order to properly make disciples. Keith Phillips made a sobering point when he said, "A mature disciple must teach other believers how to live a life pleasing to God and must equip them to train others to teach others. No person is an end in himself. Every disciple is part of a process, part of God's chosen method for expanding His kingdom through reproduction."[19]

Those who teach the truth and live a lie contradict the truth they preach and teach and do great harm to the tender hearts of the hearers. Dr. Phillips made another profound observation in his book when he said, "Discipleship is the only way to produce both the quantity and the quality of believers God desires."[20] Christian educators must see themselves as disciplers, and negligent disobedience is the result of their not seeing and acting as disciplers. According to Jesus, making disciples and teaching go hand in hand (Matthew 28:19-20).

---

19. Keith Phillips, *The Making of a Disciple* (Los Angeles: World Impact Press, 1981), 21.
20. Ibid., 22.

Christian Leadership. Where there are leaders, there are followers. Leaders model, and church leaders are examples to the flock (1 Peter 5:2-3) of growing toward the image of Jesus Christ (Romans 8:29). Church leaders who simply lead in planning, promoting, presenting, projecting, and presiding are guilty of negligent disobedience. Church leaders who do not intentionally seek to make, mark, mature, and multiply disciples are partially obeying the Great Commission. The biblical qualifications found in 1 Timothy 3 and Titus 1 strongly suggest that it is important to assess the character of a leader. Leadership skills are necessary, but because of the ultimate goal of leadership, which is be shaped into the image of Jesus Christ, character is more important than skills. Leaders must see themselves as not over or above the flock but living among the flock as paragons, or examples, to the flock. It is imperative that they understand that the ultimate goal is to nurture those whom they are responsible to shepherd, to grow from regeneration, through sanctification, to glorification. Jeff Iorg, in his book on leadership, rightly stated when he said, "The simple goal of becoming more like Jesus should be the ultimate goal of every leader."[21]

Therefore, leaders must be spiritually mature saints who model Christ's character as they grow in grace and in the knowledge of Jesus Christ while influencing growth and maturity in the Body of Christ. They must be spiritual parents able to reproduce in others what has been produced in them. They model making a disciple by being disciples, which requires making a tremendous investment in the lives of those they lead. Dr. Costas said, "To disciple someone is to establish a personal relationship with the view of shaping his entire life."[22] Discipleship must not be just a ministry of the church—it must be *the* ministry of the church. Every Christian leader must view discipleship as *the* ministry. A leader is on his or her way to a destination. There is a destiny in view, not just a duty to perform. To accomplish a task or project is noteworthy but it is not the ultimate goal of leadership.

---

21. Jeff Iorg, *The Character of Leadership* (Nashville, Tennessee: B&H Publishing Group, 2007), 21.
22. Orlando E. Costas, *The Church and Its Mission* (Wheaton, Illinois: Tyndale House Publishers, 1974), 74.

Worship. When we worship in Spirit and in truth, it will enhance making, marking, maturing, and multiplying disciples. Mindless and meaningless worship is unproductive to the process of making disciples. When scriptural truth is missing or marred in our corporate gatherings, God is not exalted and disciples are not edified. Corporate worship is essential to discipleship development (Hebrews 10:24-25). The worship experience should make sense (1 Corinthians 14:6-25). It should be a supernatural encounter with the Holy, but it must not be nonsensical. The unbeliever may not fully understand why we respond in praise like we do but ought to sense our profound love for God. When disciples pray, praise, and preach there should be a sense of wonder. Oh, how they love Jesus! Where there is authentic worship, the true worshipper will leave the encounter with the Holy with a glow and a go (Exodus 34:35; Isaiah 6:1-9). Worship leaders need to spend time with God before they lead in worship. They must become disciplers who have been with God before they can help the worshipper to encounter God. It cannot be orchestrated. It must be the outworking of an in-working presence and power of the Holy Spirit (Colossians 3:16-17).

To encounter God, our worship must be vertical, which means it must be God-focused. We cannot encounter God if our worship is horizontal, or man-focused. Everything in worship must be about God. We sing, pray, and preach unto the Lord. The Lord is the audience of one. If we are to encounter Him, we must forget about ourselves and focus on Him. Worship God (Revelation 19:10; 22:8-9). The worship ought to be about our decreasing in order that God might increase. Worship is praise and praise is worship. Both are the worshippers' lofty opinion of God, who is worthy. Worship and praise belong to Him alone. He is before, beyond, and above all creation. We exist, live, and move because of Him. We know and are known because of Him. He alone sustains, supports, and supplies our needs for human survival (Acts 17:23-28). The life that we have and enjoy is the breath of His life, which is borrowed breath. The disciple of Christ is doxological by nature (Ephesians 1:3-14); we can't help but to praise Him—it is in our nature. Because of what has taken place in us, we are worshippers and praisers. Worshipping is negligent disobedience when it does not lead the worshipper to engage in making, marking, maturing, and multiplying disciples. Those who are responsible for creating a climate for experiencing the presence of God must see themselves as doxological disciples. And all disciples must understand their responsibility in preparing themselves through private worship for public worship (Psalm 34:1-3; 100:1-5). Both of these passages talk about private and public worship. Private worship made public praise possible. The worshippers brought the fire with them to the public worship.

Out of the Audience. We are worshippers, but we are also witnesses. Jesus did not send us to go into the church but into the world. We really don't need a church building to do what God has called us to do, which is to go make disciples. We have been commissioned by Christ, the Head of His church to engage in a "go ye" ministry, not a "come ye" ministry. The challenge of the Christian church is getting the members out of the audience and into the army—the "salvation" army, if you please. Making disciples is the business of the entire church, not just for the elite few, but for every member of Christ's body. Every member is called and sent to invest in relationships in order to be a reflection of Christ, reproducing disciples for Christ. However, we must not neglect worship. Before we go into the world, we must go by the church for corporate as well as private worship.

Worship reminds us that we are powerless without God. To gain strength for combat on the battlefield, we soldiers of the Cross and followers of the Lamb need some "R&R" restful rejuvenation that happens when we authentically encounter God in worship. Discipleship without doxology will disable our effectiveness as disciple makers. Those who authentically worship work for God and join Him where He is working. True worship helps us to properly assess who God is and who we are not in relation to His holiness (Isaiah 6:1-9). True worship helps us to make proper adjustment to involve ourselves in "co-missions." Worship that does not inspire making disciples is negligent of the worship leader or worshipper or both.

To worship God and not become "*a living sacrifice, holy and acceptable to Him, which is your spiritual worship*"[23] is incomplete obedience, which is probably no worship at all. I am afraid of worship that is styled as a "Holy Ghost party" or getting your "praise on," for it sounds like horizontal worship more than vertical. It sounds like it is more about us than God. The pivotal question is, can we truly worship God while living in negligent disobedience to the Great Commission? God desires and demands obedience.

---

23. The Holy Bible: See Romans 12:1 (paraphrase)

The Second Thought: Beyond the Meaning to Jesus' Model of Making a Disciple

This second thought captures the totality of this book: What is a disciple? You are probably thinking that the second thought should have been covered first, in chapter 1. The definitions of the word *disciple* are, in my estimation, surface meanings. To define a disciple as merely "a follower or pupil of a leader or teacher" is biblically inadequate. There is a distinction between Jesus' disciples, Plato's disciples, and John the Baptist's disciples. Christian disciples must not be defined in secular or religious terminology. We are subject to wrongly define what it means to be Christ's disciples when we broadly define the term; we are then more likely to make discipleship optional in the life and experience of the Christian. Jesus did not *define* a disciple; He *described* a disciple.

If we look at the meaning before we examine the model, we will fall short of the true nature of what it means to make disciples. Jesus was the paragon discipler. He was aware of other forms of discipleship, but He called His disciples out from among the other forms. The men He called were ordinary men who would be involved in reaching the world with the Gospel of grace. These men would become transformational disciples. They would be dynamically changed in order to change their world. Perhaps the spirituality of the reader of this book is the result of the obedience of these ordinary men who responded in salvation to the call to follow Jesus. We would be wise to look at Jesus' model before we give meaning to discipleship. The following is the model that I see in Scripture that describes making a disciple and will be the core of this book: ***"A disciple is an obedient follower of Jesus, relating, reflecting, and reproducing disciples."*** His followers were called "disciples" before they were called "Christians": *"And in Antioch the disciples were first called Christians."*[24]

In his book *Not a Fan*, Kyle Idleman said that mere disciples are fans. Jesus had disciples, and, unlike disciples, fans or mere followers have ulterior motives for following Jesus. They are uncommitted to the person and seek only the privileges. Jesus described mere followers as those who *"seek [Him], not because [they] saw the signs, but because [they] ate of the loaves and were filled."*[25] They wanted the manna but not the Son of Man, who was the Living Bread. Why do you follow Jesus? Your answer to this query will determine if you are a fan or an authentic follower (disciple) of Christ. The cost to be a fan of Christ is nothing; but the cost to be a follower of Christ is everything. Look at Peter's statement in Matthew 19:27 (NIV): *"We have left everything to follow you! What then will there be for us?"* There is some ambivalence in his statement, but he does give a distinction between the fan and the authentic follower (disciple). The authentic follower of Christ is not following to get, but to give. As we look back at John 6, Jesus identifies those who are members of the fandom crowd. They are those who are apostate in nature: *"From that time many of His disciples went back and walked with Him no more."*[26] Judas Iscariot was a prime example of a fan (John 6:70-71). Fans attach themselves to the church but not to Christ. They are in church, but not in Christ, and Christ is not in them (John 17:20-23). Fans belong to the organization but are not in the organism. They embrace the teachings of Jesus without knowing the Teacher personally.

Fans are so close but yet so far away, which is tragically unfortunate. They are in Jesus' circle and in the congregation of the church of Christ, but are not authentic followers of His. Fans are tasters of the heavenly

---

24. The Holy Bible: Acts 11:26c (ESV)
25. The Holy Bible: John 6:26 (NKJV)
26. The Holy Bible: John 6:66 (NKJV)

gift and partakers of the Holy Spirit, tasting the good Word of God and powers of the age to come, but they fall short of knowing Christ personally (Hebrews 6:4-6). What a sad picture of apostasy—lost in the house of God because they are not members of the household of God (Ephesians 2:19). Being in the house of God is not the same as being in the household of God. In the house of God, you are just a guest; a weed among wheat. But, in the household of God, you are family. You are organically related. You are not Judas—living and functioning among the disciples as a fan but not as an authentic follower of Jesus.

Members of the Multitude

And seeing the multitudes, He went up on a mountain, and when He was seated His disciples came to Him.[27]

I would like to suggest that there is a distinction here that is probably overlooked by the reader. And seeing the *fans*, Jesus went up on a mountain, and when He was seated *His followers* **came to Him**. They came to Him because they had previously come to Him when Jesus had initially called them to Himself (Matthew 4:18-22). No doubt they came to Jesus in response to His message: *"Repent, for the kingdom of heaven is at hand."*[28] There is no mention of an emotional or a dramatic response—they simply came to Him. Saul of Tarsus's coming to Christ was more dramatic (Acts 9:1-9). But these fishermen simply came to Him. But was it simple? Was there more to it than meets the eye? It wasn't just His teachings and occasions of healing that drew His followers. They were drawn to Him. It appears that the multitudes came for the wrong reasons. They came to get from Him, not to give themselves to Him. Jesus' disciples would need discipling because they had much to learn about the ministry and destiny of their Lord. But their coming to Him was transformational. They dropped their nets and entered into dramatic relationships with the incarnate God. The

---

27. The Holy Bible: Matthew 5:1 (NKJV)
28. The Holy Bible: Matthew 4:17 (NKJV)

call to come to Jesus was a call to enter into discipleship, delivering them from a "mega" type of fandom.

Evidence of authentically coming to Jesus is believing and abiding in Him. A noted past salvation experience is not as important as present-tense believing and abiding in Jesus. If you believe in Christ in the now, it is because you have believed in Him in the *then*. Evidence of birth is life. Since you are alive in Christ, it is obvious you have been born again. The actual time and day is not as important as the present reality of new life in Christ. The apostle Paul spoke of his Damascus Road experience before the Jerusalem crowd and King Agrippa (Acts 22:6-21; 26:12-18). Paul had a past experience, but the rest of the apostles did not appear to have one. They simply left what had them occupied, and followed Jesus. However, they were just as saved as Paul was.

One can be satisfied and comfortable in the crowd, especially when the preacher and the preaching tickle the ears of the hearer (2 Timothy 4:3-4). Crowds gather where there is no call to holiness, just a pursuit of happiness; no call to righteousness, just relevance; no call for repentance, just acceptance; no call for godliness, just a promise of the good life and the American dream; no call to suffer for righteousness's sake; just a life of no suffering. The itching-ear multitude wants a cross-free gospel. The purpose of the fandom crowd is mostly self-serving as they diligently seek their best life now rather than the kingdom's agenda. For fans, the abundant life equates to materialistic gain and not spiritual growth. They have a faith that does not look up to Christ, but down to them. What matters most is their comfort rather than His redemptive cause. While we are fascinated with the crowd, Jesus reminds us that for the few authentic disciples, the gate is small and the road is narrow (Matthew 7:13-14). It is not the gate and road of cheap grace, but of costly grace. It cost the Father His Son, and the Son His life. As well, it costs the true disciple his life (Luke 14:26-27; John 3:16). The faith of fans of Christ is merely intellectual faith, but the faith of authentic followers of Christ is trusting and obedient faith—a faith that produces transformation and not mere intellectual assent.

An Obedient Follower

We have talked about an obedient church, and now we turn our focus to an obedient follower—and not just a follower but an **obedient** follower of Jesus. Jesus' call to discipleship is deeper than just a student following the teachings of the teacher. It is the response of an obedient faith that is anchored in the sayings, doings, and being of the Teacher. It is possible to be a Christian practitioner and not be a Christian. It is possible to believe in God and not be a believer. One would agree that this sounds paradoxical. *"You believe that there is one God. You do well. Even the demons believe—and tremble!"*[29]

The devil and his demons are theists. In fact, they are monotheists. They have a reverent fear of God, and they even have a correct Christology. They know who Jesus Christ is and what He has accomplished for mankind. The devil is not confused about God, Jesus, and the Holy Spirit. His aim, however, is to confuse man and drive him to become atheistic and agnostic. The devil knows the truth that has been told of him: that he is the father of lies, and what he knows about God makes him an effective liar.

"And the evil spirit answered and said, 'Jesus I know, and Paul I know; but who are you?'"[30] *"Now it happened, as we went to prayer, that a certain slave girl possessed with a spirit of divination met us, who brought her masters much profit by fortune-telling. This girl followed Paul and us, and cried out, saying, 'These men are the servants of the Most High God, who proclaim to us the way of salvation.'"*[31]

---

29. The Holy Bible: James 2:19 (NKJV)
30. The Holy Bible: Acts 19:15 (NKJV)
31. The Holy Bible: Acts 16:16-17 (NKJV)

In order to keep man in bondage, Satan does not want man to know the truth. To be the deceiver, Satan must know the truth (2 John 7). He is the chief of the anti-Christ spirits and teachers. And he does not want the world to know what he knows about Christ. So he stands against the truth about Christ, who is God's only way, only truth, and only life (John 14:6). Man is God's focus for redemption and reconciliation; therefore, Satan is envious of him. He wants man to remain under condemnation and darkness until he himself is cast out unto utter darkness with the demons and with those whose names are not in the Book of Life (Revelation 20:10, 14-15; 21:8).

Satan has intellectual faith in the Gospel. He knows that the Gospel "*is the power of God unto salvation*" (Romans 1:16, KJV). His deceptive plan is to keep mankind ignorant of its power. Ever since he was informed of his demise (Genesis 3:15) at the Cross, he attempted to divert Jesus from reaching Calvary. He knew that the blessing pronounced in Genesis 12:1-3 had to do with the Blessed One—Jesus, Mary's baby. So he set out to make Israel a curse instead of a blessing to all nations. But God preserved His blessed plan of redemption through an undeserving people, and this treasure in earthen vessels was kept until it landed in the womb of Mary (Isaiah 9:6). Then Satan employed King Herod to *destroy Jesus* at two years old before He could get to Calvary. Then Satan attempted to *disqualify Jesus* by getting Him to yield to his temptations. Then Satan attempted to *discourage Jesus* from going to Calvary through His friend Peter; and finally, while Jesus was hanging on the cross, Satan attempted to *dissuade Jesus* to abort His divine mission by coming down from the cross (Matthew 2:16; 4:1-11; 16:23; 27:38-44).

Beyond Belief

An obedient follower is one who has obeyed the Gospel. And an authentic disciple is rooted in obedience while entering into the process of discipleship. This lifestyle of obedience starts with obeying the Gospel. What does it mean to obey the Gospel? Are we speaking of earning salvation through obedience? Don't we just have to simply believe and then we are saved and obedience follows in sanctification? This school of thought suggests that intellectual assent is sufficient to attain salvation, and belief in the facts of the Gospel is enough to save one. This premise makes disciple making optional. You can be a Christian without being a disciple. The unhealthiness of the church is the result of not going beyond belief to an obedient faith. The Scriptures command obedience as necessary for salvation.

"For God so loved the world that He gave His only begotten Son, that whoever believes in Him should not perish but have everlasting life."[32]

"He who believes in the Son has everlasting life; and he who does not believe the Son shall not see life, but the wrath of God abides on him."[33]

"But they have not all obeyed the gospel. For Isaiah says, 'LORD, who has believed our report?'"[34]

"In flaming fire taking vengeance on those who do not know God, and on those who do not obey the gospel of our Lord Jesus Christ."[35]

Some would suggest faith is not the *cause* of our salvation but the *result* of salvation. Faith does not happen *outside* of salvation but, rather, *inside* salvation. Faith is a gifting inside of salvation. *"For by grace you have been saved through faith, and that not of yourselves; it is the gift of God, not of works, lest anyone should boast."*[36] Let me enter this mystery of the doctrine of election and human freedom with these feeble comments. If a sinner is

---

32. The Holy Bible: John 3:16 (NKJV)
33. The Holy Bible: John 3:36 (NKJV)
34. The Holy Bible: Romans 10:16 (NKJV)
35. The Holy Bible: 2 Thessalonians 1:8 (NKJV)
36. The Holy Bible: Ephesians 2:8,9 (NKJV)

responsible for his unbelief (John 3:18, 36), then he must have something to do with his belief. Could it be that faith is not something that the sinner does to gain salvation, but the acknowledgment that he is unable to do anything but trust what Christ has done on his behalf? Therefore, faith is an act of surrender. *"Nothing in my hand I bring, simply to thy cross I cling."*[37]

The apostle Paul expressed his total dependence on the cross of Christ this way: *"But God forbid that I should boast except in the cross of our Lord Jesus Christ, by whom the world has been crucified to me, and I to the world."*[38] To believe is really to trust, not to merely acknowledge and declare, but to rely on that and on who you know. Therefore, believing is not something that the sinner does, but the belief is on whom the sinner depends.

It was not what the ancient Noah built and acknowledged that saved him and his family, but on what he and his family depended upon (Genesis 7:7; Hebrews 11:6-7). Please notice the element of obedience in the faith of Noah. He obeyed God and entered by faith into a boat of which its seaworthiness was unknown. God designed the instrument of their salvation and they had to simply surrender themselves to His designed plan of salvation. This sounds like a prototype of God's ultimate plan and means of salvation in Christ. There is no glory to be declared and claimed by the one who trusts in the saving efficacy of another. We must only glory in the cross of Christ, the means of salvation through His blood.

Listen to these wonderful words of the apostle Paul as he defined *belief* as "trusting." It warms my heart to hear these words applicable to every disciple's story. Listen!

"In Him also we have obtained an inheritance, being predestined according to the purpose of Him who works all things according to the counsel of His will,

---

37. "Rock of Ages, Cleft for Me," by Augustus M. Toplady, 1740-1778, in the *United Methodist Hymnal* (Nashville, TN: The United Methodist Publishing House, 1989), Hymn #361.
38. The Holy Bible: Galatians 6:14 (NKJV)

that we who <u>first trusted</u> in Christ should be to the praise of His glory. In Him you <u>also trusted</u>, after you heard the word of truth, the gospel of your salvation; in whom also, <u>having believed</u>, you were sealed with the Holy Spirit of promise, who is the guarantee of our inheritance until the redemption of the purchased possession, to the praise of His glory."[39]

Being obedient to the Gospel is placing your trust in the Christ of the Gospel. It is a trust-type believing. However, faith is not void of intellectual assent because the content of the Gospel (the facts) is essential to the Gospel message that must be heard (Romans 10:8-15; 1 Corinthians 15:1-8). The word of faith must precede saving faith. God, who acted in redemptive history through Christ, is the object of saving, justifying faith. There is also the emotive element of faith. The emotions are stirred upon hearing the Gospel (Acts 2:37). Through the spoken Word, the Holy Spirit touches the emotions and draws the sinner from darkness to light. The sinner does not decide on his or her own to come to Christ; the sinner is drawn through the work of the Spirit (John 6:44; 16:5-15). Sinners demonstrate faith by trusting in Jesus for salvation, recognizing that they are not trustworthy. Sinners cannot depend upon themselves for salvation and, therefore, they must have faith in the atoning work of Christ which leads them to turn to Christ from sin. This is where faith and repentance coordinate in accomplishing salvation. The dynamic of this faith makes necessary faith as a gift from God. Trusting in God is evoked by God.

Then there is the volitional element of faith, which is the surrendering of the human will to the Divine will. A surrendered life is a life that says "Yes, Lord!" It is a life of pleasing the Lord—a life lived under the lordship of Christ, which is the core desire of the disciple. Jesus is Lord and Savior over a life that is surrendered unto the lordship of Christ, and this happens upon coming to Christ. *"If anyone comes to Me and does not hate his father and mother, wife and children, brothers and sisters, yes, and his own life also,*

---

39. The Holy Bible: Ephesians 1:11-14 (NKJV) (personal emphasis added)

he cannot be My disciple."[40] All relationships will stand in the secondary position when compared to Christ as Lord. The primacy of Christ over persons, possessions, and purposes is pertinent to being a disciple (Luke 14:26-33). In this volitional element of faith, the will is surrendered, obedience is planted in the heart, Christ becomes Lord, and, thus, disciples are born. Disciples are born when the sinner dies. This is not a physical death, but it is death to sin, and resurrection to life. Dietrich Bonhoeffer said it well: "When Jesus calls a man He bids him come and die."[41]

Much may not be understood by the believing sinner as he or she comes by faith to Jesus, but at that initial point, he or she has been crucified with Christ (Galatians 2:20). This has taken place in eternity and in two histories—Christ's and the sinners'. The life of the disciple begins at the new birth. It is not optional. It is not secondary to salvation. It is not another level of the Christian life. It is not the Christian becoming more spiritual and disciplined. The health of the church depends on how we view making disciples. Is it post-salvation or salvation? Another related question that needs exploring that I feel affects the health of the church is, "Is intellectual assent sufficient for salvation?" Is factual faith in the Gospel enough and faith obedience unnecessary? How we answer these queries will determine the health of the church—for an undisciplined grace will be evidential in an undisciplined Christian life.

Jesus Is Lord

When is He Lord, and is it necessary that He be Lord? There is great debate inside Christianity on the subject of the Lordship of Christ. It is related to an obedience-led faith versus an intellectual-led faith as a means of salvation. Some view Jesus as Savior, and not Jesus as Lord, as the only thing that matters in salvation. The Lordship of Christ is too demanding. Faith in Christ as Savior is enough for salvation to take place. In the

---

40. The Holy Bible: Luke 14:26 (NKJV)

41. Dietrich Bonhoeffer, *The Cost of Discipleship* (New York: Simon & Schuster Publishers, 1959), 99.

sanctification process, the Lordship of Christ can develop into the thinking and life of the believer. One of the most used passages to lead a sinner into a saving relationship with Christ is Romans 10:9 (NKJV), which reads, *"If you confess with your mouth the Lord Jesus and believe in your heart that God has raised Him from the dead, you will be saved."* Paul told his fellow kinsmen that salvation was available to them if they viewed Jesus as Lord. He did not say as Savior, but Lord. It was essentially important that the Jews view the carpenter's son as Lord. This denoted that Jesus was God and the promised Messiah. And, it is important that we Gentiles have the right perspective of who Jesus is, but not equally so, because the Jews had other issues with Jesus. During His lifetime on earth, Jesus was rejected by the Jews, and they crucified Him (John 1:11; 19:15-16). Paul clearly declares that declaring Christ as Lord is necessary to salvation. In essence, Paul is saying that you cannot deny that Jesus is Lord and then believe salvifically. This stance will get in the way of your salvation and block you from the grace of God. Paul further said to the Gentile who wanted to be saved in Acts 16:31 (NKJV), *"Believe on the Lord Jesus Christ, and you will be saved, you and your household."* The Lordship of Christ was vital to the preaching ministry of the apostles (Acts 2:21, 34, 36; 3:14-16, 19; 5:30-31; 10:36).

Jesus is Lord. But to what extent is He Lord? In deity? Or simply dominion? Can God be God without dominion? Man was given dominion, but without deity, and he attempted to seize deity through that dominion and his God-given likeness (Genesis 1:26; 3:4-6). It is not my aim at this point to pursue the fall of man but, rather, to suggest that "Jesus is Lord" could be understood as His being a "lord," having dominion without deity. But, throughout New Testament Scripture, Christ is affirmed as being Lord in the God sense, as written in the following passages:

While the Pharisees were gathered together, Jesus asked them, saying, "What do you think about the Christ [Messiah]? Whose Son is He?" They said to Him, "The Son of David." He said to them, "How then does David in the Spirit call Him [the Christ] 'Lord,' saying: 'The Lord [the Father] said to my Lord [the

Son], "Sit at My right hand, till I make Your enemies Your footstool."' If David then calls Him [Christ] 'Lord,' 'how is He [Christ] his [David's] Son?'"⁴²

Then He said to Thomas, "Reach your finger here, and look at My hands, and reach your hand here, and put it into My side. Do not be unbelieving, but believing." And Thomas answered and said to Him, "My Lord and my God!"⁴³

"This Jesus God has raised up, of which we are all witnesses. Therefore being exalted to the right hand of God, and having received from the Father the promise of the Holy Spirit, He poured out this which you now see and hear. For David did not ascend into the heavens, but he says himself: 'The LORD [the Father] said to my Lord [the Son], "Sit at My right hand, till I make your enemies Your footstool."' Therefore let all the house of Israel know assuredly that God has made this Jesus, whom you crucified, both Lord and Christ."⁴⁴

"Jesus is Lord" appropriates salvation, whether spoken or unspoken. Whether explicit or implicit, He is Lord. One thing is certain: the new nature will not allow the denial of the Lordship of Christ that is related to His deity (1 John 2:18-23). Knowing and understanding all the essential doctrines of Scripture are not requirements for being saved, but to disavow the essential doctrines and still claim to be saved is incongruent to having taken on the new nature—case in point, the denial of the Incarnation as confronted in 1 John 4:1-3. There are those essential teachings of Scripture that teach us that if one were to deny or disavow the essential teachings, then that person was never a child of God (1 John 2:19). Viewing disciple making and obedience under the Lordship of Christ as optional, and relegating it to the sanctification process, results in unhealthiness in the church and a "cheap grace" atmosphere. It will not produce spiritual parents for spiritual infants.

---

42. The Holy Bible: Matthew 22:41-45 (NKJV) [What is underlined is author's addition for emphasis.]
43. The Holy Bible: John 20:27-28 (NKJV)
44. The Holy Bible: Acts 2:32-36 (NKJV) [with emphasis added]

A Closer Look at Matthew 28:18-20

With three supporting participles, to the main verb in the imperative mood, the authoritative Lord of the church sends His disciples into their world to impact the world with the Gospel through making disciples. The flow of the passage indicates that it is about initial salvation. It is the beginning of one's relationship with Christ. He does not tell disciples to go and evangelize the world; rather, He tells them to go and make disciples of all nations. Why doesn't He tell them to go and evangelize? It is not because the Good News is not to be shared, but that it is to be shared through forming relationships. We will develop this thought more fully later in this literary work. But for now, let us take a glance at the salvific flow in the passage.

To make disciples and then mark them through baptizing them speaks to what qualifies one to be baptized. Baptism symbolizes a past experience that is testified to through water baptism. It is the disciple's birth certificate. It marks that the believing sinner has died to sin and has been raised to walk in the newness of the resurrected life (Romans 6:4). After hearing the good news, the Ethiopian wanted to know what prevented him from being baptized, and Philip answered, *"I believe"* (Acts 8:36b, NKJV). Infant baptism is not accepted in most churches because infants do not have the capacity to comprehend the Gospel in order to believe (Mark 16:16). Since baptism is to follow the making of a disciple, it indicates that a disciple is born through the new birth—not made through teaching but by the touch of the Spirit through regeneration (Ephesians 2:1-3). Then after the disciple is made and marked he is to mature through the teaching of the Word of God (1 Peter 1:22-25; 2:1-3). To teach is not simply to *know* but to *grow*. To observe is to obey the Lord in order to grow into His image (Matthew 28:20; Romans 8:29). The effectual presence of Christ's Spirit happens in obedience. Christians are not developed into disciples; disciples are developed in order to reproduce disciples. Again, we further discuss this idea of reproduction later in this book.

The Missional Church under Mandate

The person who comes to Jesus as a result of the move of the Spirit upon his or her life is changed. It is a dynamic and salvific change. It is not a philosophical change, but a born-again change that is inclusive of the mind, the emotions, and the will. Those who authentically come to Jesus do not remain the same. They become disciples of Jesus. Look again at Luke 14:26 (NKJV): *"If anyone comes to Me."* The "coming" in this passage is salvific. There is a change in relational priorities where Christ becomes preeminent in the life of the one who comes to Him. He becomes the Lord of that life, which takes place without full knowledge and comprehension. The person comes, and He changes. When water met Christ, it became wine. When the blind met Christ, they went away with sight. When the lame met Christ, they left walking. When the dead met Christ, they became alive again. When the lost met Christ, they were found. Only those who do not come authentically, leave unfulfilled. The Rich Young Ruler left his encounter with Jesus sorrowful (Matthew 19:22-26). Nicodemus left his encounter with Jesus inquisitive (John 3:9). Simon, the sorcerer who encountered Jesus through the preaching of Philip, believed and was baptized for the wrong reason. He did not want Christ; he wanted the power to do miracles—therefore, he left under judgment (Acts 8:5-24). Those who sincerely come to Jesus experience a wonderful change. Luke 14:27 reads, *"And whoever does not bear his cross and come after Me cannot be My disciple."* You cannot come after Him until you have come to Him. To come to Him is salvation, and to come after Him is service. It is doing because there is being. It is the disciple engaging in discipleship.

The implied imperative "go ye" must be obeyed by the church and her members. They are to transact Christ's unfinished business in the world. As the Father sent His Son into the world so did the Son send His church and her members into the world (John 17:18). Calvary's business was completed on the Cross. The dying Savior declared that human redemption was objectively achieved through His atoning sacrifice (John 19:28-30).

He had accomplished that which only He could do—die in the place of sinners, thereby being the means by which God was just and the justifier (Romans 3:26). One of the most thrilling and tremendous chapters in the New Testament canon is the first chapter of Ephesians, which tells us that we were saved before time, in time, on time, and beyond time. Ephesians 1 is a blessed assurance chapter that speaks of God's indestructible purpose in saving us. Nothing can thwart God's purpose and plan that He is perfecting in and through us (Romans 8:29-39). This finished work of God in Christ must be propagated throughout the world. This is the sole business of Christ's other Body—the church. Only Christ could save the world and only His church can tell of His saving grace. As Jesus was focused on the business of Calvary, so must His church be focused on Christ and Him crucified (1 Corinthians 2:2).

The church, in her quest to be relevant, is tempted to involve herself in what others can do better than what she can do, and to, therefore, neglect doing what only she can do. A multifocused church is ineffective in reaching the world through the word and ministry of reconciliation. Complexity is an enemy to simplicity. The church that is focused on making disciples and involving herself in the ministry and word of reconciliation is rarely cluttered. Christ's vision for His church is to reach the entire world with the Gospel. His strategy is for the body of believers—His church—to go into the world and make disciples. They were not to be stationary, but missionary. He did not create the church to be boxed in a building. The method for reaching the world was not by inviting sinners to church, but by inviting them to Christ through the disciple's presence and proclamation in the world. This is a "go ye" strategy rather than "come ye." Church buildings that are attractive and state-of-the-art may draw people to attend, but attractive disciples of Christ will draw people to Christ. We dare not turn our church buildings into monuments, but use them as instruments for equipping disciples to impact their world with Gospel presence and proclamation. I am convinced that we really don't need church buildings to do what God has called us to do. Sometimes, church buildings can be an impediment to reaching the world. The early church was stuck in Jerusalem. They had been commissioned, equipped, and empowered to take the Gospel into the entire world, but they were busy having church and not being the church. With a membership of about 10,000, they had become a mega-church in Jerusalem that was a growing church but not a going church. They were not missional, but God-allowed persecution made them missional (Acts 8:1-4).

The Preaching Church

There is much discussion these days on who should preach. Denominational split has occurred around who has the authority to preach the Gospel. Who has the right to preach? When you really think it through, no one has the right to preach. It is a privilege and a responsibility. While I understand God's order in the family and church (1 Corinthians 11:3), preaching is the business of the entire church. ***(I sense excommunication rising up!)*** To reach the world with the Gospel of Jesus Christ, preaching must not merely become the mission of the ordained but also the organism (Romans 10:14-15). The church must preach. As Jesus came preaching, His church must go preaching (Mark 1:14). She preaches through the Eucharist and evangel (1 Corinthians 11:26; Acts 8:4). The Gospel will never reach the world with a "come ye" strategy. It is when the church scatters, involving herself in the "go ye" strategy, that the world is reached. We need lay preachers as well as clergy preachers if we are to reach the world. We need all genders and generations involved in the evangelistic mission of the church. When we limit the Gospel enterprise to the elite few (licensed and ordained males), we hinder going into all the world making disciples of all nations. All must become domestic or foreign Gospel missionaries. If we are to reach the masses, preaching must not remain the exclusive business of the few, but the inclusive business of all believers.

Is who should preach a matter of pulpit presence? Who has the right to stand and share the Gospel behind the sacred desk? This seems to be where the tension lies. Men are guarding the holy hill while sinners are lost in the valley of dry and dead bones, needing the church to commission believers to invade the valley with Gospel presence and proclamation. Who should preach? The church must go preaching. Every member of the Body of Christ must go to their concentric circle and influence with Gospel presence and proclamation. As Jesus traveled, He preached and taught in the synagogues, on the seashore, and on the mountain. He was not stationary but missional. He preached outside more than inside the walls. He modeled preaching in season and out of season. He modeled preaching as proclamation and demonstration because He was and is the living Word. What is preaching? It is truth communicated with the intent of persuasion, spoken or unspoken. It has more to do with substance than style. Preaching is at its best when it is Christocentric and of the Holy Spirit. When preaching, the preacher must strive to decrease in order for Christ to increase.

"For we do not preach ourselves, but Christ Jesus the Lord, and ourselves your bondservants for Jesus' sake. For it is the God who commanded light to shine out of darkness, who has shone in our hearts to give the light of the knowledge of the glory of God in the face of Jesus Christ."[45]

What is the difference between preaching and evangelizing? After the martyrdom of Stephen, the apostles remained in Jerusalem and the church members scattered and evangelized as they went throughout the regions of Judea and Samaria. In Acts 8:4, the word for "preach" is *evangelize*. The leaders of the church stayed while the members of the church went preaching. This is how the Gospel spreads—the laity must carry it. The answer to the question, *Who should preach?* is that everyone must preach. The church will never reach the masses through the pulpit. The pew must take the Gospel to where they live, work, learn, and play. The pulpit is to equip the pew for the work of the Gospel ministry (Ephesians 4:11-16). We are so concerned about getting church workers to function in the

---
45. The Holy Bible: 2 Corinthians 4:5,6 (NKJV)

church that we have neglected getting witnesses into the world. We are too busy going to church instead of going to the world. Rick Warren was correct when he wrote, "I believe that you measure the health or strength of a church by its sending capacity rather than its seating capacity."[46] We were called out of darkness, made, marked, and matured as disciples and sent back into darkness with the light of the glorious Gospel shining in and through us in order to multiply disciples (Matthew 5:13-16; 1 Peter 2:9).

"As thou didst send me into the world, even so sent I them into the world."[47]

The Body of Christ and its members belong in the world. God loved the world so much that He sent His Son (John 3:16). Christ loved the world so much that He sends His church. Making disciples is not an added thing you must do as a disciple, but this is accomplished as you go about life, keeping in mind that you are in the world but not of the world (John 17:16; Romans 12:2). Disciples are ambassadors who belong to another world and represent King Jesus in a foreign world (2 Corinthians 5:20; 1 Peter 2:11). The disciple of Christ is otherworldly and his witness as an ambassador is living a life of contrast as he is being different to make a difference.

---

46. Rick Warren, *The Purpose Driven Church* (Grand Rapids, MI: Zondervan, 1995), 32.
47. The Holy Bible: John 17:18 (ASV)

The Third Thought: Making Disciples through Relationships

The implied imperative is "as you go, *relate.*" Remember that the working definition of a *disciple* is "an obedient follower of Jesus *relating*, reflecting, and reproducing disciples." The Christian doctrine of God is very interesting. It is Hebraic in that it is monotheistic: *"Hear, O Israel: The LORD our God, the LORD is one!"*[48] Yet, within the Godhead there is this interpersonal relationship between the Father, the Son, and the Holy Spirit. The Christian God is Trinitarian in nature. Three distinct persons and one God ($1 \times 1 \times 1 = 1$) is the mathematical equivalence of the Trinity. Each one is infinitely distinct, forming one God. They are not just manifestations of the one God, which would be too impersonal. And we should not attempt to explain away the three-ness and oneness of the Trinity by saying there is one person with three different names, roles, or activities. Pay close attention to this paradoxical statement: "The Godhead exists 'undivided in divided persons.'"[49] This doctrine defies reason but is the product of Divine revelation. God has disclosed Himself in Trinitarian fashion in Holy Scripture. There is this co-ality within the Trinity—co-eternal and co-equal. There is an *"us-ness"* in oneness in the Trinity: *"Let Us make man in Our image, according to Our likeness."*[50] At the baptism ceremony of Jesus, the undivided in divided persons is manifested: Jesus in the water, the Father speaking from heaven, and the Holy Spirit as the witness are distinctively present (Matthew 3:13-17). In the implied imperative found in the Great Commission, Jesus declared the three-ness in oneness when He said (in essence) to baptize them in the Trinitarian formula:

---

48. The Holy Bible: Deuteronomy 6:4 (NKJV)

49. Millard J. Erickson, *Christian Theology*, 2nd Edition (Grand Rapids, MI: Baker Publishing Group, 1998), 361.

50. The Holy Bible: Genesis 1:26a (NKJV)

"Go therefore and make disciples of all the nations, baptizing them in the name of the Father and of the Son and of the Holy Spirit."[51]

While the term "Trinity" is not used in Scripture, the teaching is certainly declared in the Old and New Testaments, and to deny this teaching harms monotheism and the sinless nature of Christ. Christ claimed to be the Son of God, thus declaring equality with the Father. He identified Himself as Yahweh in His "I Am" statements, and He received worship that only belonged to God (John 10:30; 14:6; 20:28). If He was not who He claimed to be, then He was just a sinner and, therefore, He could not have qualified to be our Savior. The Trinity is socialized theology in that there is interrelationship within the Godhead. Notice the dialogue in Hebrews 10:5-7 (NKJV):

Therefore, when He came into the world, He said: "Sacrifice and offering You did not desire, but a body You have prepared for Me. In burnt offerings and sacrifices for sin You had no pleasure. Then I said, 'Behold, I have come—in the volume of the book it is written of Me—to do Your will, O God.'"

Then in John 16:5-7 (NKJV) we read this:

"But now I go away to Him who sent Me, and none of you asks Me, 'Where are You going?' But because I have said these things to you, sorrow has filled your heart. Nevertheless I tell you the truth. It is to your advantage that I go away; for if I do not go away, the Helper will not come to you; but if I depart, I will send Him to you."

Don't you sense here the interpersonal relationship between the Son and the Holy Spirit? Inside the Trinity, they are one in essence but subordinate in function. Surely, there is socialization in the Trinity as they function in their interrelationship; however, they never act independently

---

51. The Holy Bible: Matthew 28:19 (NKJV)

of one another. It was only when Jesus became sin for us, did He sense abandonment (Matthew 27:46). God is relational inside the Trinity.

Christ Is Relational

As we look at making disciples as relational, Jesus models this for us because He entered the world to relate. He was born into a family and grew up *"in wisdom and stature, and in favor with God and men."*[52] In that high Christology passage found in the prologue of the gospel of John—the relational text:

"And the Word became flesh and dwelt among us, and we beheld His glory, the glory as of the only begotten of the Father, full of grace and truth."[53]

Jesus was in a relationship in the beginning (John 1:1-3), and now on earth, He comes to relate as the God-man to fallen man. Through the Incarnation, God enters into relationship with man. The Son of God sacrificed to relate with man. He left His exaltation for humiliation (Philippians 2:6-7). He who was rich became poor (2 Corinthians 8:9). Keep this thought in mind as you read this book: making the investment to go into the world to make disciples is costly. Jesus modeled the cost of making disciples. The Great Commandment—loving the world, loving brothers and sisters, and even loving your enemies—had a view of making disciples (John 3:16; 13:34-35; Romans 5:8-10; 1 John 4:7-11, 20-21).

The Men

Notice Jesus' strategy for reaching the entire world. He called twelve men into relationship with Himself. This was perhaps the first disciple small group. His focus was the men. We ought not to make light of this male focus strategy of the Lord. God again was on a search for man. *"Then*

---

52. The Holy Bible: Luke 2:52 (NKJV)
53. The Holy Bible: John 1:14 (NKJV)

the LORD God called to Adam and said to him, 'Where are you?'"[54] We must not think generically at this point. I know as it relates to salvation, *"There is neither Jew nor Greek, there is neither slave nor free, there is neither male nor female; for you are all one in Christ Jesus."*[55] When it comes to leadership in the home and in the church, husbands and fathers are held responsible. This appears to be the order throughout Scripture. It is not a glamorous or glorious position, but a guardian position of servant leadership under the Lordship of Christ. This position is not so much to be envied or sought after. The men in this position are the main target of the enemy who seeks to destroy the home and the church, and this is evidenced by the absenteeism of men in the home and the church. Jesus' disciples were told to follow Him and He would make them fishers of men (Matthew 4:19). I believe Jesus meant exactly what He said—fishers of men, not fishers of women. Men need to be discipled for the sake of stronger homes and effective churches. When Jesus gave the Great Commission, there was no doubt more than the eleven present which indicates that making disciples would be the business of more than the few, but the many. In fact, it is the business of the entire church (Matthew 28:16-20). Jesus modeled the Great Commission before He commissioned them. He discipled the Twelve, except one who was just a fan and not an authentic follower (Acts 1:15-26).

God with Us

Jesus as Emmanuel is God with us (Matthew 1:23). He came to relate so that He may have a relationship with us. The remote God becomes relatable. The impersonal God becomes personal. Through Jesus Christ of Nazareth, God becomes relatable. The Son of God is now the Son of Man without ceasing to be God's Son (Philippians 2:5-11). There are now two natures in the one person, Jesus, the Christ. He became flesh without ceasing to be God. In what some call the "kenosis," Jesus did not empty Himself of divinity. He simply cloaked His divinity with His humanity.

---

54. The Holy Bible: Genesis 3:9 (NKJV)
55. The Holy Bible: Galatians 3:28 (NKJV)

In order for God to relate with us, He identified with us through the Incarnation. His self-limitations were His own prerogative. There was the finite and the infinite existing in Him. He was fully God and fully man, but as man, He was more human than fallen humanity. He was utopia man, or authentic man. The God-man was necessary for fallen man to have a relationship with a holy God.

God had to send Himself on mission and ultimately become man's substitute and means of justification in order for fallen man to be in relationship with a holy and righteous God (2 Corinthians 5:17-21). God wanted His relationship with humanity restored. Sin severed man's relationship with God (Isaiah 59:2), but through Christ, we are reconciled for the sake of a restored relationship with a holy God. The Christ of Christianity is the only means for the restoration of man's relationship with God (John 14:6). God is only approachable through Christ and Him alone. Modern man does not like this only-ness, but it is corroborated by Scripture (Acts 4:8-12). God's purpose is not to make us religious, but relational, which can only be experienced in union with Christ (Colossians 3:1-4). In one's becoming a disciple, a relationship with Christ is formed (John 3:3-8; 1 John 5:11-12). Religion is a practice, but Christianity is a way of life lived in the power of the indwelling Holy Spirit (Romans 8:9-11). Moreover, Christianity is the life of Christ in the believer enabled by the presence and power of the Holy Spirit. The abundance of the disciple's life (John 10:10) is two-dimensional (Philippians 1:21; Galatians 2:20)—the resurrected Christ at home in the disciple, and the permanent power and presence of the Holy Spirit (John 14:16-18). Our relationship with Christ is the only way we can have a relationship with His Father (1 Timothy 2:5). This is truly the abundant life.

Body Life

As Christian disciples, we were chosen to do life together with other disciples of Christ. The primary social ministry is inside the Body of

Christ. As disciples, there is the vertical relationship with Christ, and then there is the horizontal relationship with one another in the Body of Christ. Through the baptism of the Holy Spirit, we became members of the one another-ness (1 Corinthians 12:12-30). Individual disciples and local congregations must understand and embrace this spiritual reality if the church is to function as designed by Christ, who is the Head of His church. Solo Christianity, or a churchless Christianity, is incongruent with the Head of the church. It is against Body life. The church as the reincarnation of Christ, the extension of His presence on earth, must understand and function as an indispensable union. In Jesus' intercessory prayer, He prayed for oneness (John 17:21), and I believe that through the baptism of the Holy Spirit, we objectively became one, and now we must subjectively function as one Body in Christ, and in order to do that, we must love one another with our giftedness.

"A new commandment I give to you, that you love one another: just as I have loved you, you also are to love one another. By this all people will know that you are my disciples, if you have love for one another."[56]

The challenge of obeying the Great Commission is a matter of loving one another in the Body of Christ, and in the world. We must have love for saints and sinners. Developing relationships must become intentional in the Body of Christ and in the world. Love is always sacrificing to achieve God's best for another person. Disciples are commanded to live beyond the norm and love even their enemies and not just their neighbors (Matthew 5:43-44). The greater need of neighbor and enemy is to know Jesus Christ as Savior and Lord. The Savior modeled what the disciples' attitude is to be toward their enemies when Paul wrote, *"For if while we were enemies we were reconciled to God by the death of his Son, much more, now that we are reconciled, shall we be saved by his life."*[57] When we go into the world with the intent to make disciples, God's love for us is to be our motivation to

---

56. The Holy Bible: John 13:34-35 (ESV)
57. The Holy Bible: Romans 5:10 (ESV)

love others (1 John 4:11). When we intentionally relate in order to make a disciple, we are expressing love at its best.

The church must be seen as an organic social group where many members comprise one Body. This organic social group is a living organism wherein the members interact with one another and share similar characteristics. This is the essence of Ephesians 4:15-16. This organic social group—the church—is more intimate than the average social groups, for it has a shared life component that originates from a relationship with Christ the Head, wherein each member shares Christ's life and His redemptive blood flows through each member of the Body. Therefore, if the question was posed as to whether or not your church is involved in social ministries, the answer is yes. Social ministry starts with loving one another, caring for one another, forgiving one another, building up one another, and serving one another in the Body of Christ. Let me debunk the so-called "social gospel." There is only one kind of Gospel that has to do with what happens on Good Friday and Resurrection Sunday. Any other gospel is not the Gospel (Galatians 1:6-11). The Gospel is social in that it is good news to a sinful society. So, we must go into the world relating and making disciples for Christ. However, the disciples' relationship in the one another-ness equips and enables the church's mission in and to the world.

The Body of Christ's Social Response to the World

The church is sent into the world primarily to make disciples. The church's social responsibility in the world is not to provide goods and services, but the Gospel of salvation. The church is not to become a kind of social agency. Our special attention should be to one another without neglecting the needs of the unchurched (Galatians 6:10). It is dangerous for the church to neglect doing what only she can do and participate in what other groups can do much better than her. The church offers Christ not mere charity. The world is in danger when the church neglects her mission in the world, which is to make disciples through the preaching of the Gospel. Although she has been influential in establishing schools, hospitals, fighting for social justice, and the like, what she can do best is be the church. In the epistles to the church in Rome, the apostle Paul does not confront the social plight of his race under Roman oppression—he just declares his obligation to preach the Gospel in Rome:

"I am under obligation both to Greeks and to barbarians, both to the wise and to the foolish. So I am eager to preach the gospel to you also who are in Rome. For I am not ashamed of the gospel, for it is the power of God for salvation to everyone who believes, to the Jew first and also to the Greek."[58]

What a powerful statement. Paul was saying that what he owed the world was the preaching of the Gospel of grace. It had changed him. And he believed that it was the answer for the world. His assertion was that some were ashamed of the Gospel and, therefore, engaged in preaching things other than the Gospel of the cross of Christ (1 Corinthians 1:17-23; Galatians 1:6-9). A gospel void of the Cross is no gospel at all. Following a social-liberation gospel that does not lead to a gospel unto salvation (spiritually) is like gaining the world but losing your soul (Mark 8:36). It is a deliverance that leaves the delivered empty (Matthew 12:43-45). A social-liberation gospel that does not lead to making a disciple leaves the liberated person in a worse condition. He becomes self-sufficient and begins to think that he has no need for Christ. The church must not turn to a different gospel to appease the hearer. There is no power to change man from the inside out unless the Gospel is preached. In our relationship with the world, disciples of Christ must go into the world and preach and demonstrate the Gospel.

"How then will they call on Him [the Lord] in whom they have not believed? And how are they to believe in Him [the Lord] of whom they have never heard? And how are they to hear without someone preaching? And how are they to preach unless they have been sent? As it is written, 'how beautiful are the feet of those who preach the good news!'"[59]

---

58. The Holy Bible: Romans 1:14-16 (ESV) [with author's emphasis]
59. The Holy Bible: Romans 10:14-15 (ESV)

The aforementioned passage is relegated to the called, the preacher who stands behind the so-called sacred desk. But could this observation be too pinched, too pressed into a narrow exclusive group of proclaimers? As aforementioned, to limit the proclamation of the Gospel to the few and not the many is to hinder reaching the entire world with the Gospel of grace. All who have "feet" must carry the Gospel to their world where they work, live, play, and learn. The world needs a preacher in order to hear. The preacher, the evangelist, and the witness must share the Gospel in every form of communication.

(At this point, I would like to thank the reader for allowing me these parenthetical remarks. I will now continue the discussion on Body Life.)

The Indicative Perspective

The factual view of the church is its relationships in the organism. The church is more than a family. It is more than a relationship between brothers and sisters in Christ. We are members one of another. Let me repeat—the church is an organism. Listen closely to the apostle Paul's words: *"For as in one body we have many members, and the members do not all have the same function, so we, though many, are one body in Christ, and individually members one of another."*[60] This interdependence is intrinsic to Body life. It is intimacy on the deepest level of life. This oneness in us-ness is mysterious in origin and function. It is Trinitarian in nature: One God in three Persons, and one church with many members. Local congregations are microcosms of the Body of Christ. We are related as brothers and sisters in the church, but more so as members one of another. Oh, how I wish we would grasp this indicative perspective! Our indispensable relationship as members of Christ's Body is clearly delineated in 1 Corinthians 12:

If the foot should say, "Because I am not a hand, I am not of the body," is it therefore not of the body? And if the ear should say, "Because I am not an eye,

---

60. The Holy Bible: Romans 12:4-5 (ESV)

I am not of the body," is it therefore not of the body? If the whole body were an eye, where would be the hearing? If the whole were hearing, where would be the smelling? But now God has set the members, each one of them, in the body just as He pleased. And if they were all one member, where would the body be?[61]

The baptism of the Holy Spirit is not an imperative that we must seek. It is an indicative we must realize. The indwelling and baptism of the Holy Spirit is the Christian's reality (1 Corinthians 12:13; Romans 8:9). As Christians, it is the filling of the Spirit that is commanded (Ephesians 5:18). It is unthinkable for people to consider themselves Christians but they are not connected with other Christians in a congregation of the Body of Christ. A Christian who desires to function solo as a Christian is thinking too lofty of himself or herself (Romans 12:3). It is wrong to think of the church as being in your heart, because one can live in disassociation from other members of the Body of Christ. But that is not the Christian's reality because Christians were baptized into the one another-ness. We trifle with membership in the Body of Christ and devalue the mystery of our relationships within the Body because of spiritual ignorance.

"Do you not know that you are the temple of God and that the Spirit of God dwells in you? If anyone defiles the temple [the church] of God, God will destroy him. For the temple of God is holy, which temple you are."[62]

"Temple," here, refers to the Body of Christ, not the individual bodies of the Christians. The Christian's physical body is also a temple—it is a temple of the Holy Spirit (1 Corinthians 6:15-20). But in chapter 3 of Corinthians (the verses referenced above), Paul is referring to the temple of God, which is the corporate Body of Christ, and he states that it is dangerous to trifle with the church. Examples of trifling with the church include, but are not limited to, being inoperative with our giftedness, non-supportive, complaining, gossiping, causing division, conflict, sinful behaviors, envy, strife and unfaithfulness. Such behaviors cause the church

---

61. The Holy Bible: 1 Corinthians 12:15-19 (NKJV)

62. The Holy Bible: 1 Corinthians 3:16-17 (NKJV) [emphasis added]

to be ineffective and inefficient. The church is so related that if one member suffers, all members suffer—whether good or bad (1 Corinthians 12:26).

Being members of the holy temple of God requires us to think soberly about our relationship as members of the Body of Christ.

Relational Discipleship

Making disciples is a matter of relating and not an inconvenience or just enrolling in a course. Although involvement in groups such as discipleship groups, growth groups, small groups, or accountability groups can result in relationship building which can lead to making disciples if the "win" is the goal: "We win when each member grows in relationship with Jesus, being, doing, thinking like Him, influencing growth and maturity in the Body of Christ."[63] Christlikeness is to be the direction and destination of all growth in discipleship. The disciple will want to be like Him, do like Him, and think like Him in order to effect growth and maturity in the Body of Christ, and relational growth will facilitate reaching this destination. Growing in relationship with Jesus happens best when disciples live in the one another-ness, and this is how we win. Healthy Body life is essential to making disciples, and small groups are an intricate component of healthy Body life. Personal growth can be facilitated and measured best through small discipleship groups. This was Jesus' model and strategy for making disciples to reach the world. He spent relational time with twelve men, and some time with just three. He shared His life with them and made an investment in them for the sake of the world.

Permit me to recite the working definition of a "disciple" that Jesus described. A *disciple* is "an obedient follower of Christ, *relating*, reflecting, and reproducing disciples." The relational God, who sent His Son into the world to reconcile fallen humanity unto Himself, sends His church, His Body, the reconciled community, back into the world to participate

---

63. Fred Campbell, *The Win: Knowing and Pursuing Our Destination* (Nashville, Tennessee: Townsend Press, 2017).

in sharing the Word and ministry of reconciliation through relational discipleship. Each member of the reconciled Body of Christ is to engage in making disciples. If the world is to be reached, each one must reach one. Relational discipleship of sharing the Gospel through witnessing is a natural methodology. Through one's social environments, and interrelationships where you work, live, play, and learn, with intentionality and love, you can share the Gospel. As you take interest in others with loving concern for the total man and woman in the context of their lost-ness, you can love them and lead them into a relationship with Christ.

The Family and Relational Discipleship

The purposeful God established the family as the first institution. The family was meant to serve as the foundation to all other institutions that would be formed. The whole human race was affected by the disobedience of Adam's family (Romans 5:12-14). The nation of Israel would be situated on Abraham's family, and the faith of father Abraham blessed the whole nation. However, the unfaithfulness of Abraham created conflict between two people groups even unto this present day. As the family goes, so go the other institutions. The health of the church is directly related to the health of its families, and the health of the families is influenced by the health of the leaders of the church, especially the health of the pastor's family. Among the qualifications for church leaders, pastors are called to be the husband of one wife, to manage their homes well, and to train their children to be submissive. Church care is related to home care (1 Timothy 3:2-5). According to the apostle Paul, failure at home will render the pastor ineffective at church. Because we measure success in unspiritual terms, we can think that our churches are effective when they are spiritually unhealthy.

The Pastoral Family Paradigm

The pastor is the steward of the family and the church, and, as a steward, he is the example and model of Jesus to his primary flock—the family, as well as to the secondary flock—the church. In managing his household, the pastor/husband/father is making disciples as he pioneers the faith and offers himself up as servant. He gives himself for the sake of the well-being of his wife first, and then the children (Ephesians 5:23, 25). As head, the pastor/husband/father sets the pace toward the image of God's Son. To love his wife is to nurture her faith toward the image of Christ and not contradict the Word that cleanses (Ephesians 5:26). As the pastor/husband nurtures his wife he is also nurturing himself because the two of them have become one flesh (Ephesians 5:28). As the pastor/husband models Christ, he must see his wife as part of the glorious body that is to be presented spotless and without wrinkle in holiness before the Lord. This is discipleship taking place in the home with the pastor/husband loving his wife as Christ loved the church and he sacrifices in order to achieve God's best for her. The pastor/husband knows that this love may cause him to bleed as Christ bled for His church. The pastor/husband knows that love is meant to be inconvenient; therefore, he must come to the end of himself for the sake of the relationship with his wife.

Plural oneness is expressed through Christian marriage, and the Trinity and the church are typified in Christian marriage. Christian marriage is a microcosm of the church. It reflects the mysterious and miraculous union of Christ and His church. The one another-ness in marriage is continued in the one another-ness in the Body of Christ. The reason why God hates divorce is because it damages the truth about Him and His church (Malachi 2:16). Divorce tells an untruth about the truth of the indispensable, inseparable union in the Body of Christ. God's best is for the husband and wife (and children) to be conformed into the image of Christ (Romans 8:29). This is the end product of discipleship—to be like Jesus. We follow Him to become like Him.

Discipleship in the Marriage

Certainly, loving your wife is key to being able to disciple her. However, the apostle Peter gives us some practice points. *"Husbands, likewise, dwell with them with understanding, giving honor to the wife, as to the weaker vessel, and as being heirs together of the grace of life, that your prayers may not be hindered."*[64] Marriage was instituted by God for the godly and the Christian, and those outside of His purpose cannot adequately model the purpose. Marriage will not be needed in heaven because its purpose is fulfilled on earth (Matthew 22:30)—for through holy matrimony, God desired to speak of His relationship with Israel and His church. In Christian marriage, the husband represents Christ—the Head of the church—and the wife represents the church.

The Bible does speak of unequally yoked marriages (2 Corinthians 6:14). A submissive wife has an opportunity to be used by the Holy Spirit to influence an unbelieving husband (1 Peter 3:1). It is noteworthy that the wife is not told to love her husband, but to submit to her husband who loves her like Christ loved the church. This was extremely different in the first-century world—to love your wife. When the wife feels that she is prioritized above everyone and everything—except the Lord—she feels special. She does not feel like she is an afterthought. When she is valued for who she is and thanked for what she does, she feels special. When the wife is treated with care and tenderness, she feels special. All of this creates an atmosphere for discipleship. With the two (the husband and the wife) becoming one flesh—one marital person who are heirs together of the grace of life—discipleship is a mutual process. Therefore, praying with each other and for one another is invaluable to the couple's spiritual growth. The husband is the provider, protector, priest, and prophet, and he must nurture his wife so that his relationship with God will not be hindered.

---

64. The Holy Bible: 1 Peter 3:7 (NKJV)

The following are Peter's practical points on how to disciple your wife. First, seek to understand her. Your wife's complexity as a woman calls for you to live with understanding. She is uniquely different from you. To understand her is to be present, to be a patient listener, to be a prayer partner, and to be a practitioner of nonsexual intimacy (such as sharing in the housework). Second, honor your wife. She is special and you are to let her know that she is special as your wife and mother to your children (if you have children). You are to make your wife feel special by letting her know and demonstrating to her that she comes second only to the Lord.

The Christian Family

What makes a family Christian? Is a family considered a Christian family because there are Christians in the home? Is it Christian because it embraces the Judeo-Christian values? Is a family or home Christian in name only or also in nature? There are families with Christians, and there are Christian families. Christian families are innately Christian; they are Christocentric. Moreover, the family is Christian when it engages in the cause of Christ and becomes the primary place to make a disciple. In the Christ-centered family, Christ is Lord and His mission is the mission of the family. The Christian family and church understand and function in a symbiotic relationship, which presupposes that the family is ideally Christian with a Christian marriage according to Scripture (Ephesians 5:31). The heterosexual church demands a heterosexual marriage. Couples consisting of two husbands or two wives are incongruent with Christ's church (Ephesians 5:22-33). The church is proclaimed in Scripture as "she" and the head of the church, Christ as "he."

The family is Christian when Christian parents produce godly seed, which is what Paul describes in Ephesians 6:4 (NKJV) that the father should take the lead in producing godly seeds: "*And you, fathers, do not provoke your children to wrath, but bring them up in the training and admonition of the Lord.*" I believe this is done when the children observe the father's love for Christ and their mother. Children are attracted to Christ by their parents' authentic relationship with Christ and one another. The D6 (Deuteronomy, chapter 6) family is an Old Testament model of a Christian family. The father assumed the lead in teaching the children by inundating the home with obedience to the commandments of God. The discipleship process in the Jewish home was intentional and driven by love for God. It was not mere religious instruction, but very much relational. *"You shall love the LORD your God with all your heart, with all your soul, and with all your strength."*[65] You can sense that the Jewish home was the primary place for the family to develop their faith and walk with God. It did not begin with the larger gatherings but in each individual household. The Word of God was worn (bound) on their hands and posted on their homes, and they were instructed to live out the word as they sat in their houses and walked by the way, which is the best way for parents to facilitate discipleship in the Christian home.

When the apostle Paul admonished fathers to not discourage their children (Colossians 3:21), he no doubt had in mind Christian hypocrisy. When the church father and mother do not embrace their role as disciple makers in the home, relationship with Christ is not encouraged, and they are only leading their children to church but not to Christ. Parents must not delegate their responsibility to disciple their children to the children and youth ministries of the church. The home and the church must become partners in the spiritual development of the children. It is incumbent upon the local congregation to see the family as the primary ministry of that congregation. The "yellow" home and the "red" church must become orange. There must be a symbiotic relationship between the home and the church in order for both to experience health. The church must become para-family, and the home must become para-church.

---

65. The Holy Bible: Deuteronomy 6:5 (NKJV)

The Wife as a Disciple Maker

She comes from his side to function at his side in making the family the primary place to make disciples.

And the LORD *God caused a deep sleep to fall on Adam, and he slept; and He took one of his ribs, and closed up the flesh in its place. Then the rib which the* LORD *God had taken from man He made into a woman, and He brought her to the man. And Adam said: "This is now bone of my bones and flesh of my flesh; she shall be called Woman, because she was taken out of Man."*[66]

With this new creation, there was no battle of the sexes. However, conflict between Adam and Eve was ushered in at the fall of man as one of the consequences of sin (Genesis 3:16). Pain in childbirth, which is another consequence, remains, but the pain between husband and wife is removed in the new creation when the old is passed away and the new has come (2 Corinthians 5:17). It is at that point that the disciple's perspective of marriage becomes different from that of the old creation. There is equality in the home and equal value in Christ (1 Peter 3:7). Husband and wife were both created in the image of God and re-created in the image of Christ, and although they are both equal in essence and in Christ, they are each subordinate in function. God holds the husband/father in the Christian home responsible for living out the purpose of the home's being the primary place to make disciples. When the family strays from its purpose, God is still asking, "*[Adam], where are you?*"[67] And, like in the case of Adam, fathers are consequential to the function and dysfunction of the family.

The function of the wife is to respect her husband in his God-given responsibility as leader of the home (Ephesians 5:33). He is responsible for modeling being conformed to the image of God's Son. I have named this as the overarching responsibility because all other responsibilities are

---

66. The Holy Bible: Genesis 2:21-23 (NKJV)
67. The Holy Bible: Genesis 3:9 (NKJV)

contextualized within this one. The husband is the protector—physically, mentally, emotionally, and spiritually. He is the provider of the family's needs, both financially and materially. He is the priest—the intercessor before God on behalf of the family. He is the prophet—God's spokesman in and to the family. That is a lot of responsibility for the husband, but his wife is his partner and helper in all of the areas of responsibility. God said to Adam and to every husband and father that *"it is not good for the man to be alone."*[68] He needs an equal as a helper. A woman who is less than he or who is objectified will not help him as his wife. He needs a wife who submits to her husband as unto the Lord—a wife who has the Lord in her view. This suggests that the home is a Christ-centered home—a home where the husband is busy being like Christ, and the wife is busy responding like the obedient church.

The obedient wife is obedient to the Lord in her response to her husband's functioning under the Lordship of Christ. It is in her obedience to making the home the primary place to make disciples that she functions as a Proverbs 31 wife and mother. She has great worth and her husband will treat her as valuable to the fulfillment of God's purpose for the family. She is profitable, strong, giving, and she sacrifices for the good of the family. She adorns herself for the sake of her husband, and she is not a distraction in public. She is a wise and watchful wife. She is productive and blessed by her children and praised by her husband. Above all she loves the Lord, and this is obvious to all. This type of wife is indeed a helper to the husband and father who is charged with leading his family toward the image of Christ.

The Foundation

"If the foundations are destroyed, what can the righteous do?"[69]

I can imagine God's displeasure when the saints are living in conflict and quandary. When we, who are the salt of the earth and the light in

---

68. The Holy Bible: Genesis 2:18 (NIV)
69. The Holy Bible: Psalm 11:3 (NKJV)

the world, are living in a dark age, I believe God weeps (Luke 19:41; Ephesians 4:30). The prophetical company of believers ought not to live as reactionaries who do not understand the times and do not know what to do (1 Chronicles 12:32). The query "What must we do?" ought not be the Christian's query. We may not have all the answers, but as Christians we do have the answer to the human plight, plunge, and predicament—Jesus, the last Adam (Romans 5:12-17). The first Adam was consequential to the human predicament, but the last Adam is consequential to the human redemption. We, who are born-again believers, not only have the answer but we are examples of the answer as witnesses to the power of the Gospel unto salvation (Acts 1:8; Romans 1:16). We ought not to be reacting to what is happening in the world, and we are to be more than proactive—we are to be pre-active. As believers, our response to the matters of life come from the fact of our predestination (Romans 8:28-30). We don't live in the context of the surprised but in the context of the sovereignty of God (Isaiah 14:24, 27; 55:11). We are pre-active when we stay the course and are not swayed by the current events of the world. The call for relevance is for the church to adjust to what is happening in the world today, and we must understand that the message and the ministry of the church are always relevant. To attempt to make the Bible relevant through re-contextualization is to pre-textualize the Bible.

Satan is humanity's enemy and he wants to destroy the human race. Although he probably rejoiced when Noah's generation was destroyed, I believe he lamented when he saw grace extended to humanity in the ark floating upon the waters with eight human beings safe within. The angels that fell with Satan were not extended grace and no redemption awaits them—only damnation. Some are already chained while others await their assignment to hell with their leader, Satan (Jude 6; Revelation 20:2-3, 7-10). Again, Satan hates humanity and, through deception, he wants to blind and keep humanity in darkness (2 Corinthians 4:3-4; Revelation 12:9). His strategy is to destroy the foundation of humanity, which is the family.

He started by deceiving Adam's family, and he has been after families ever since the fall of the first family. His primary focus is the Christian family that has been commissioned to reach the human family with the Gospel of grace in order to depopulate hell (John 3:16-18; 2 Peter 3:9]).

The Body of Christ—God's Church—is well-established in the world for Christ as the chief cornerstone, and she rests on the foundation of the apostles and prophets (Ephesians 2:20), but her effectiveness in the world is greatly impaired when families within congregations of the Body of Christ are dysfunctional. Congregations are made up of families, and the health of the church is related to the health of the families. Therefore, it is no surprise that Satan is focusing on destroying the congregation's witness in their communities by destroying the families in the congregations. The unholy trinity: Satan, the flesh, and the world's sinful system, are militating against the effectiveness and even the survival of the family. Christian marriages are on Satan's cross-hairs, and pastoral marriages are especially targets of the unholy trinity.

The fact that the pastor's marriage is under Satan's attack gives credence to its fundamental significance to the health of his congregation. The pastor is the key man. He is the bishop. He not only oversees budgets, buildings, board members, and structures, but he oversees souls. However, the pastor's marriage is his ministry, and there is a vivid and vital correlation between the pastor's family and the health of his congregation. He must not separate what goes on at church and what goes on at home. Again, I would like to refer to the apostle Paul's inspired statement in 1 Timothy 3:4-5 (NIV) because I think it shows the correlation between the home and the congregation: *"He must manage his own family well and see that his children obey him, and he must do so in a manner worthy of respect. (If anyone does not know how to manage his own family, how can he take care of God's church?)"* When this qualification for pastoring is a constant reality, it encourages the families of the congregation to do the same. When this is true, the pastor and his family oversee the core of the congregation—

marriage and family. Some pastors may not be aware of the fact that the condition of his marriage and family is vital to the spiritual health of the congregation. Satan is aware of this fact.

"Therefore take heed to yourselves and to all the flock, among which the Holy Spirit has made you overseers, to shepherd the church of God which He purchased with His own blood."[70]

This pastoral warning is personal and somewhat private before it is public: *"take heed to yourselves."* What Paul is saying to the Ephesian elders/overseers, as well as to pastors in the twenty-first century, is *watch yourselves*. I believe he is charging pastors to pay attention to their relationship with God, and, for those who were and are married, their relationship with their wives and children. The walk with God must take priority over their work for God. Both Enoch and Noah were noted for their walk with God (Genesis 5:24; 6:9). The effectiveness of the work is determined by how intimate the pastor's walk is with God. The pastor must not confuse his pastoring and preaching with his personal relationship with God. Pastoring and preaching can become self-glorifying if the pastoring and preaching are not the results of the pastor's relationship with God. Pastors need to walk with God in order to come to the end of self or else ministry can become a means of self-validation, and in the pursuit of self-validation, the pastor can sacrifice his marriage and family, making them casualties of the pastoral ministry. Pastors can gain the world, popularity, positions, prosperity, and pleasures and lose their marriages and families. It is not in the interest of heaven that a person becomes a great pastor and a poor husband. The enemy of the ministry must not become the marriage nor should the marriage become the enemy of the ministry.

If the pastor and wife would view marriage and ministry symbiotically, it would remove the antagonism. The pastor must guard his relationship with God and his wife and children by prioritizing it this way: God is first,

---

70. The Holy Bible: Acts 20:28 (NKJV)

his wife is second, the children are third, and the congregation must come in fourth. The question is this: How is this done? The answer is by the *"equipping of the saints for the work of ministry, for the edifying of the body of Christ."*[71] This is really a discipleship process. Christians must get out of the audience and into the army. They must get out of the pew and into the purpose of the church in the world. The laity must become fully engaged in the ministry at home and out in the world through the church. Every member and couple in the church must embrace this priority: God first, spouse second, children third, and church fourth.

Although some marriages may start out wrong, they are transformed and end well. Unfortunately, this is not often the case. If a marriage starts out wrong, it will likely end wrong. The manner in which marriage is entered into is important. Many who are Christians enter into marriage not realizing that the marriage is more for God than for the couple. God wanted to use the marriage to say something about Himself and His church. This understanding is invaluable to starting well. However, sadly, there are Christian marriages that start out well but end in divorce. How does this happen? Especially when the man and the woman who have been united in holy matrimony are both born-again believers who are indwelt with the same Holy Spirit and who believe in and love the Word of God. What causes them to get to the point where they are contradicting Christ and His church by going through a divorce? How did they get to this place? No doubt that many ask themselves the same question: How did we get here? Especially when they did not intentionally set out to get to this horrible place in life. I think that the demise of the marital relationship is caused by a gradual decline; it is not something that happens overnight.

Satan has his eye on the marriage from the very day vows are exchanged before the Lord in the company of witnesses. He waits on his two friends—flesh and the world's system—to create an atmosphere and attitude that would enable alienation to enter into the marriage. Satan waits on self-

---

71. The Holy Bible: Ephesians 4:12 (NKJV)

will and self-centeredness to reverse the one flesh metamorphosis that occurs when man and woman come together and are no longer two but one. They begin to think selfishly and make life all about themselves and their happiness. They exchange the word "we" for "me." Interdependence has returned back to independence. That is flesh. Then Satan waits on the world's system to have a greater influence on the marriage than the kingdom of God has on it. The world's system acts as termites eating away at the marriage, which is the foundation of the family and church. The foundation begins to crumble and deteriorate in such a subtle and unrecognizable way that when it becomes apparent, it is almost irreparable. That which can destroy the marriage appears benign, like eating from the *"tree of the knowledge of good and evil."*[72] What was so wrong with eating from the Tree of the Knowledge of Good and Evil? Why was God so restrictive? Fast-forwarding to the modern era—we live in a democratic system that says we ought to be able to love and marry whomever we desire. Our democracy gives us the right to redefine marriage. What is wrong with conforming to this democratic culture? Why can't we simply redefine marriage? These queries are examples of the termites that are destroying marriage as foundational.

Innocent intrusions into the marriage can simply be a career path that militates against the marriage. Among those intrusions could be children who slip into second place, distancing the couple from one another, and/or the pursuit of materialism that can cause marital neglect, both of which lead to having a house but not a home. As already mentioned, the church and its ministries can militate against the marriage and family when the family finds itself in competition with church events. The undisciplined pursuit of anything in this world that hinders godly growth in the marital relationship carries with it the danger of rendering one or the other unattractive which can negatively affect the intimacy in marriage.

---

72. The Holy Bible: Genesis 2:9 (NKJV); see Genesis 3:5.

"Do not be conformed to this world, but be transformed by the renewal of your mind, that by testing you may discern what is the will of God, what is good and acceptable and perfect."[73]

The world's system does not always appear sinful, immoral, or unethical. It may be seen as right and accepted because it seeks rightness. The world's system leads away from God and His purpose in the world, so it is always antithetical to the kingdom of God, which seeks righteousness (Matthew 6:33). A democratic society probably dignifies humanity more than a totalitarian society, but at the same time its sinful system is anti-man, for it causes man to fall short of God's intent for man (Romans 3:23). The worldview is generated by the satanic world system. Democracy that gives rise to the worldview is facilitated by the system.

"For we do not wrestle against flesh and blood, but against principalities, against powers, against the rulers of the darkness of this age, against spiritual hosts of wickedness in the heavenly places."[74]

The focus of these demonic powers is Christian marriages and families. Satan is more concerned about foundations than superstructures. No matter the superstructure or how splendorous it is, it cannot stand or remain without the foundation. Going back to the subject of divorce, the tragedy is that Christians divorce each other without realizing that it is not the other person that causes the divorce, but rather it is the *"powers, rulers of darkness, and spiritual hosts of wickedness in heavenly places"* that are the real cause of the divorce. If one or both persons were to remarry, the next marriage will also be exposed to the same sinful system of the world. In most cases, when Christians divorce they are in line with the devil's program. *"The thief does not come except to steal and to kill and to destroy. I have come that they may have life, and that they may have it more abundantly."*[75] Divorce—the death of a marital person. It is the destruction

---

73. The Holy Bible: Romans 12:2 (ESV)
74. The Holy Bible: Ephesians 6:12 (NKJV)
75. The Holy Bible: John 10:10 (NKJV)

of a relationship that was to mirror the Trinity and the church. Divorce robs the world of this relational witness.

God has placed the family in the place of priority. Horizontally, marriage and the family are purposed to be in primal place. While this is the most natural place to engage in relational discipleship, it is the most neglected and seemingly difficult place to make a disciple. The husband and wife are to be second only to God, and the children are only to be third to their parents. More than likely, when this order is violated, God is not in first place. Discipleship should be the life-blood of the marriage and family. The ministry of the church should be the family. When God is in first place in the marriage and family, instances of divorce will be rare.

The Fourth Thought: Making Disciples through Reflection

The implied imperative is as you go make disciples through reflecting the image of God while you relate, remember that "a disciple is an obedient follower of Christ, relating, reflecting, and reproducing disciples." The process of discipleship was modeled for us by Jesus. Any definition that we come up with must spring from His example of making a disciple. If we do not observe His definitive description of disciple making, we will fall short of healthy Christian growth and healthy church growth. As He related, Jesus revealed the essence of His being to the disciples. Please note that He was not a mere reflection of the Father; He revealed the Father. Jesus Christ is God's self-disclosure of Himself. The heavens **declare** the glory of God (Psalm 19:1); mankind **reflects** the glory of God (Genesis 1:26); but Jesus **reveals** the glory of God (John 1:14). God exposed Himself in a very personal way. The invisible God became visible. The unknown God became knowable. The distant God became near. The transcendent God became touchable.

The General Revelation of God

The universe speaks of the existence of God. God is exhibited through nature. The Scriptures declare this truth, but an orderly cause-and-effect universe exegetes and exposes God as Creator. You cannot get something from nothing. The existence of the universe is not found in its own existence. The universe is not self-existent. It did not give birth to itself. The cosmos cannot be explained through thoughtlessness. It is irrational to come up with a cosmos without rationality. Chaos is irrational. Our universe is not a matter of illogical existence. There is a divine designer that has superimposed His will upon the origin and sustainability of the universe.

"Long ago, at many times and in many ways, God spoke to our fathers by the prophets, but in these last days he has spoken to us by his Son, whom he appointed the heir of all things, through whom also he created the world. He is the radiance of the glory of God and the exact imprint of his nature, and he upholds the universe by the word of his power."[76]

We will look again at this passage, but, for now, it is clear that through the universe God is not without a witness. The universe declares the existence and glory of God through creation. Only the unintelligent claim that thought originated from thoughtlessness [Psalm 14:1]. R. C. Sproul simply stated that "the visible world is like a mirror that reflects the glory of its Maker."[77] The earth did not produce itself. There is no such thing as "Mother Nature" as to rule out the Creator (1 Corinthians 10:26; Psalm 24:1; Genesis 1:1). The Creator stands above and beyond nature. He predates His universe. He exists within Himself. He is self-existent. He exists within His own eternity. He transcends time and space. There isn't a where-ness or then-ness with God, just is-ness. Through His creation, He makes Himself known. He glorifies Himself through His universe. The visible reveals the presence and power of the invisible (Romans 1:20-23). The complex universe and all its beauty demand a thoughtful Creator that alone is worthy of glory (Psalm 27:19). It is unthinkable to suggest that cosmological naturalism is the answer for the existence of the universe. Nature is incapable of self-creation. The forces of nature are unable to create order and design. Nature cannot act independent of itself. It is passive in that it is acted upon. It can only affect without thought, but not create. Nature needs a master.

---

76. The Holy Bible: Hebrews 1:1-3a (ESV)

77. R. C. Sproul, *Essential Truths of the Christian Faith* (Carol Stream, Illinois: Tyndale House Publishers, Inc. 1992), 4.

In an impersonal way, the heavens declare the glory of God. The invisible Creator is visible through creation, but not in a personal sense. The anthropological revelation of God is more personal than botany, zoology, and astronomy. While a thoughtful, impersonal universe bespeaks a personal Creator, humanity relates more vividly to the personhood of God.

Image Bearers

We turn to the Scriptures for our understanding of this higher revelation of God that is more reflective in nature than revelatory.

And God said, "Let the earth bring forth living creatures according to their kinds—livestock and creeping things and beasts of the earth according to their kinds." And it was so. And God made the beasts of the earth according to their kinds . . . and everything that creeps on the ground according to its kind. And God saw that it was good. Then God said, "Let us make man in our image, after our likeness."[78]

Please note that mankind is created after the personhood of God. Persons beget persons. God created other creatures, but He only created man in His image. Although God is not a human being, He is a Being. He is not an impersonal force or energy let loose in the universe as first cause; rather, He is a Divine Being, self and preexistent, saying "let there be," and there was what had never been. The existence of humanity is not through a process of evolution from some lower kind but, rather, the higher transcendent Kind—the Supreme Being. The existential purpose of humanity is to bear the image of God. It takes eternal and existential beings to accomplish this purpose—the Divine and the human being must have likeness. What is this likeness? It cannot be a visible and physical resemblance. This likeness is in selfhood. As living souls, man gains awareness of self—*I am*. Animals and plant life exist without being. The recognition of individuality in man's among-ness is unique to man. It is

---

78. The Holy Bible: Genesis 1:24-26a (ESV)

self-consciousness. Although there is plurality, there is selfhood. I am man. I am a member of the human race as self. I am interdependent, but never independent. Selfhood is sickened in self-centeredness. Healthy selfhood is not a matter of selfishness and narcissism. But man can say I am man. He or she is conscious of self. However, God is the unique self-existent one. He is I Am that I Am.

Moral consciousness is also God-likeness. Rational man mirrors the sovereign God. God's will shall be done. And man may choose to obey or disobey the will of God. He has moral freedom but not freedom from the consequence of his choices. Man is morally responsible, as Adam and Eve sadly discovered (Genesis 3:1-24). It is nonsensical to think that mankind originated from a primate. Non-persons could not produce persons. Living beings did not come to be through a big bang (Acts 17:27-29). As human beings, we have kinship with the Supreme Being. Our nearness to God is found in personhood. We are God's offspring, not mere creatures. Therefore, we are moral creatures with the ability to think and make decisions. As His offspring, we have self-determination. Idols are an affront to the living God who has personhood (Romans 1:18-25). God has no substitutes. He demands glory from nature and man. He wants declared and demonstrated glory. For man to worship nature or man is to blaspheme the name and nature of God. However, man is the highest expression of deity. He was created to give God glory. He was created to personalize God, making Him more than some higher power void of personhood. Through the Incarnation, God honors humanity and redeems mankind. I will say more about this phenomenal intrigue later.

Marred Image

Humanity merely reflects the image of God, and Jesus is the exactness of that image. He is the revelation of God. More than nature or man, Jesus, through His humanity, is the exact image of God. Nature is an inadequate revelation of the divine, and man falls short of the glory of God due to sin. Nature vaguely declares the glory of God, and the image of God is seriously marred in man. Because of sin, man has not totally lost the image, but falls short of the image. His depravity has done serious damage to the Godlikeness. To say that there is nothing good in man is not quite true. There is an image in man that God seeks to restore back to its ought-ness. Why does He seek man? Why did He become man? Why did He die in the stead of man? Why did He plan human redemption even before He created man? Why does He want to spend eternity with man? Is it something to do with being created in the image of God? The sanctity of life is found in being created in that image. *"Whoever sheds the blood of man, by man shall his blood be shed, for God made man in his own image."*[79] To say that there is nothing good in man is not good theological anthropology. Man may not be good enough, but the Godlikeness in him causes God to reach out to him in grace.

"What is man that you are mindful of him, and the son of man that you care for him? Yet you have made him a little lower than the heavenly beings and crowned him with glory and honor. You have given him dominion over the works of your hands; you have put all things under his feet, all sheep and oxen, and also the beasts of the field, the birds of the heavens, and the fish of the sea."[80]

Maybe it should be said that there is nothing good enough in man that would justify him before a holy God, apart from the atoning blood of Jesus. Yes! He is totally unable to plead his own case before a righteous Judge. *"The Lord is not slack concerning his promise, as some men count slackness; but is longsuffering to us-ward, not willing that any should perish, but that all should come to repentance."*[81] Mankind cannot place demands on a just God. Like the Jews, we stand under the rightness of the law as guilty sinners (Romans 3:9-20). The apostle Paul argues the impossibility of the moral law to aid mankind toward being in a right relationship with

---

79. The Holy Bible: Genesis 9:6 (ESV)
80. The Holy Bible: Psalm 8:4-8 (ESV)
81. The Holy Bible: 2 Peter 3:9 (KJV)

the Father. The relationship has been broken and cries for atonement to be made on mankind's behalf.

"But your iniquities have made a separation between you and your God, and your sins have hidden His face from you so that He does not hear."[82]

"God presented Christ as a sacrifice of atonement, through the shedding of his blood—to be received by faith. He did this to demonstrate his righteousness, because in his forbearance he had left the sins committed beforehand unpunished."[83]

There is no human existence without the image and likeness of God resident in human clay. In the breath of God comes the image and likeness of God, and man becomes a living soul in the image and likeness of God. Ray S. Anderson makes this astonishing statement: "If the imago Dei is essential humanity—even if expressed as correspondence to rather than identity with divine being—we must affirm its continuity through the fall: each person who is a sinner is also human. The biblical teaching seems to entail that sinners, even in their total depravity, remain human and are dealt with as such by God in judgment and in hope."[84]

How can God the Father abandon His created sons and daughters? He does not. He becomes like them in order that they might become like Him [John 1:14]. God becomes man without ceasing to be God so that the sons and daughters might become new creatures through Christ.

"Therefore, if anyone is in Christ, he is a new creation. The old has passed away; behold, the new has come."[85]

---

82. The Holy Bible: Isaiah 59:2 (NASB)
83. The Holy Bible: Romans 3:25 (NIV)
84. Ray S. Anderson, *On Being Human: Essays in Theological Anthropology* (Grand Rapids, Michigan: Wm. B. Eerdmans Publishing Co., 1982), 72.
85. The Holy Bible: 2 Corinthians 5:17 (ESV)

"But when the fullness of time had come, God sent forth his Son, born of woman, born under the law, to redeem those who were under the law, so that they might receive adoption as sons."[86]

The doctrine of the Incarnation dignifies humans created in the image and likeness of God. It makes possible the redemption of man. There was no divine plan for the angels that fell (Jude 6). God does not become an angel; He becomes a man, and comes and dwells among man revealing the Father and the truth about God and man through an act of grace. God chose to make Himself known. In the Incarnation, God shares our humanity in order to share Himself with humanity. Also, the Incarnation makes possible Christ's substitutionary death. Simply put, our redeemer was our kinsman. All the sacrifices for sin prior to Christ were insufficient (Hebrews 9:11-14, 26-28; 10:1-10). His atoning sacrifice in the place of sinners is sufficient for all times and for all sinners who will place their faith in the God who acted exclusively in Jesus Christ.

"For our sake he made him to be sin who knew no sin, so that in him we might become the righteousness of God."[87]

"Nor was it to offer himself repeatedly, as the high priest enters the holy places every year with blood not his own, for then he would have had to suffer repeatedly since the foundation of the world. But as it is, he has appeared once for all at the end of the ages to put away sin by the sacrifice of himself. And just as it is appointed for man to die once, and after that comes judgment, so Christ, having been offered once to bear the sins of many, will appear a second time, not to deal with sin but to save those who are eagerly waiting for him."[88]

The marred image is restored in man when he becomes a new creation in Christ (2 Corinthians 5:17-21). Christ in the disciple is the new man who no longer falls short of the glory of God (Romans 3:23). Christ, the

---

86. The Holy Bible: Galatians 4:4-5 (ESV)

87. The Holy Bible: 2 Corinthians 5:21 (ESV)

88. The Holy Bible: Hebrews 9:25-28 (ESV)

meditator, makes up the shortness through His cross, reconciling man back into relationship by His atoning blood. Now the glory is restored, but it is not complete (2 Corinthians 3:18; Romans 8:28-30; 1 John 3:1-3). Remember that authentic disciples are more than fans; they are obedient followers of Christ reflecting the image of God. As the aforementioned passages indicate, the way back to the image of God is being conformed to the image of God. Although humanity bears the image of God natural to mankind, they cannot bear the image of God in a supernatural way unless they be like Jesus. Christ is authentic man, and if salvation has to do with human recovery, then man needs to be transformed into the image of the Son of God. If the image of God was lost in the first Adam, it must be gained in the second Adam.

"For as by a man came death, by a man has come also the resurrection of the dead. For as in Adam all die, so also in Christ shall all be made alive."[89]

The resurrection in the future must first be the resurrection in the present. We must be buried and raised with Christ in the existential before we can experience resurrection in the eschatological.

"For if we have been united with him in a death like his, we shall certainly be united with him in a resurrection like his. We know that our old self was crucified with him in order that the body of sin might be brought to nothing, so that we would no longer be enslaved to sin."[90]

All human beings innately have the mark of the image of God through their humanness. But without the image of the Son of God, mankind will never return to authentic humanity. To reflect the glory of God, the glory of Christ must be in us. It is an unveiled glory that witnesses to the truth about God through Christ's glory within us.

"But when one turns to the Lord, the veil is removed. Now the Lord is the Spirit, and where the Spirit of the Lord is, there is freedom. And we all, with

---

89. The Holy Bible: 1 Corinthians 15:21-22 (ESV)
90. The Holy Bible: Romans 6:5-6 (ESV)

unveiled face, beholding the glory of the Lord, are being transformed into the same image from one degree of glory to another. For this comes from the Lord who is the Spirit."[91]

The process begins in regeneration, through sanctification, to glorification. Glory that began in Christ, continues through the ministry of the Holy Spirit, and consummates in glorification is human recovery from falling short of the glory of God.

The Godlikeness of humanity is not the moral nature of God being reflected. The absence of that nature is what mars humanity. Human sin is the problem, and as a matter of fact, it is the cause of all that is wrong in the world. All have sinned and come short of the moral nature of God. And there can be no affinity with God without reconciliation with Him who is holy, righteous, just, and good. There is a divine and human dilemma in this unreconcilable relationship. God and man are as far apart as the East is from the West. The answer is *"that God was in Christ reconciling the world to himself, not imputing their trespasses to them, and has committed to us the word of reconciliation."*[92] Jesus is exclusively the way back into relationship with God (John 14:6). It is a particular way, it is a narrow way, and it is the only way. It took one man to lead humanity astray, and it will take one man to lead humanity back into relationship with God (Romans 5:12-21).

The passage above strongly suggests inherent sin through the one man Adam, while not believing that there is inherent righteousness through the one man, Jesus. It is not my intention to discuss the challenge in the passage, but to simply point out that both men are consequential in human history. In fact, they are ultimately consequential. All that has gone wrong and that has gone right in the world and in the world to come stems from these two men. I believe this is the essence of the aforementioned passage.

---

91. The Holy Bible: 2 Corinthians 3:16-18 (ESV)
92. The Holy Bible: 2 Corinthians 5:19 (NKJV)

Conformed to Christ's Image

With regard to reflecting when we say that a disciple is an obedient follower of Jesus—relating, reflecting, and reproducing disciples—the disciple reflects the moral nature of God. A disciple is able to reflect the moral nature of God because of the new nature he or she possesses because of the permanent, powerful presence of the Holy Spirit. The call to be holy as God is holy is a call to be who you are as a disciple of Christ (1 Peter 1:13-16). Disciples are set apart because of who they are and whose they are: they are new creatures, and they are God's possession. In holiness, God is other and above. We are like Him when we reflect His otherness and His apart-ness.

"But you are a chosen race, a royal priesthood, a holy nation, a people for his own possession, that you may proclaim the excellencies of him who called you out of darkness into his marvelous light."[93]

"Beloved, I urge you as sojourners and exiles to abstain from the passions of the flesh, which war against your soul. Keep your conduct among the Gentiles honorable, so that when they speak against you as evildoers, they may see your good deeds and glorify God on the day of visitation."[94]

Disciples of God are saints of God and they are not of this world. Saints of God are otherworldly (John 15:18-19; Romans 12:1-2). God is supremely different in salvation, and He made us different to make a difference in a world of sameness. God is holy and pure by nature. He does what is right because He is the standard of what is right. The Decalogue (Ten Commandments) is an expression of the moral nature of God. Therefore, the Ten Commandments cannot be abolished or ignored. Although they are not a means of salvation, our inability to keep them makes us aware of our need for a Savior. However, the impossibility of achieving salvation through the Law does not suggest that it is not to be

---

93. The Holy Bible: 1 Peter 2:9 (ESV)
94. The Holy Bible: 1 Peter 2:11-12 (ESV)

obeyed. The significance of the Incarnation again is found in the fact that Jesus (as our substitute) came and fulfilled the Law for our sakes (Matthew 5:17-20). This is why it is important to be found in Him and not found outside of Him (Philippians 3:8-9). All the laws—ceremonial, dietary, and moral—were fulfilled through Jesus Christ. However, the moral law is completely obeyed in Jesus, demonstrating His divine nature, and it must not and cannot be ignored by those who are partakers of God's nature (2 Peter 1:4). Obedience to the moral law is not a means of salvation, but it is obedience through sanctification (1 John 2:3-6; 3:7-10). The motivation for obeying the commandments is love, not fear. Love for God and others will lead to obedience and service (John 13:34, 35; 14:15; 1 John 5:3). Commandments spoken in these passages do not reference the Ten Commandments, but we are not exempt from obeying the moral law of God.

Inside the moral nature or attributes of God is goodness. He is intricately good. He is perfectly good. He is good and everything He does is good. His behavior flows from His being (James 1:17). God is pure light and there is absolutely no darkness in Him (1 John 1:5). This relates to holiness and righteousness. Wrongness cannot belong to God. He is always just. The Almighty cannot be accused of being unfair. However, paradoxically, when He gives us grace, He is actually being unfair to us because we deserve justice, and if He were fair, we would experience His just wrath revealed against us (Romans 1:18). There is nothing in man that demands God's goodness toward him. Goodness is always a matter of grace. God's goodness manifested in the believer is always done in the context of His purpose (Romans 8:28).

Inside the goodness of God is His love, grace, mercies, and long-suffering. Within the moral nature of God are the characteristics of love, grace, mercies, and long-suffering. He is love, grace, mercy, and patience in the noun sense before in the verb sense (1 John 4:8; Psalm 116:5; 1 John 4:7-21). A disciple reflects God in that he is a spiritual relative of God. It is also his nature to love before he behaves in love. He loves because he has been loved—it is innate to his new nature—and he loves because it is the fruit of the root of his new being.

"By this we know that we love the children of God, when we love God and obey his commandments. For this is the love of God, that we keep his commandments. And his commandments are not burdensome."[95]

"A new commandment I give to you, that you love one another: just as I have loved you, you also are to love one another. By this all people will know that you are my disciples, if you have love for one another."[96]

Although man is created in the image of God, he needs more than his creature-ness—he must become a new creation (2 Corinthians 5:17) to love like God has loved. The love that belongs to God is rooted in the new birth and is expressed through the Fruit of the Spirit (Galatians 5:22-23) in the power of the Spirit (Ephesians 5:18). The Fruit of the Spirit is a reflection of the character of God and is necessary to guard against the misuse of spiritual gifts (1 Corinthians 12–14). Love is basic to the Fruit of the Spirit, and love is basic to spiritual gifts (1 Corinthians 12:31).

God gives grace and mercies through His goodness. Through grace, God gives what is undeserved, and through mercy, God does not give all that is deserved. He suffers long in holding back His wrath and judgment. For instance, although the wages of sin is death and part of God's judgment upon mankind, He extends life through healing in order that the lost might come to salvation, and in order that the disciple may continue to live out his God-given purpose on earth. God's mercies are new every morning because life is allowed to continue. Then God is merciful in the life of the saint when physical life becomes so painful that God takes the saint out of this world to be with Him.

---

95. The Holy Bible: 1 John 5:2-3 (ESV)
96. The Holy Bible: John 13:34-35 (ESV)

A note about sickness and death: sickness and death were not God's purpose for mankind. Sickness and death are a result of sin. Death is an enemy of God's purpose, which is why death was defeated on the Cross and will be the last enemy (1 Corinthians 15:26) destroyed. Through the shed blood of Jesus at Calvary, death was given a moral wound from which it would not recover, and a Code Blue was called on death. Death could not take the life of Jesus—who is not just the giver of life, but who *is* life (John 10:18).

The period of life between birth and death is a manifestation of God's patience extended to people through grace and mercies. The human companions of goodness and mercy are the long-suffering of God (Psalm 23:6) and are available to the saint and sinner (2 Peter 3:8-13). Time itself is God's goodness and mercies between eternity past and eternity future.

The disciple's characteristic of patience is a reflection of God's patience. As God is and has been patient with us, we are to be patient with one another (Ephesians 4:2; Colossians 3:12-13). Reflecting this characteristic of God in a world absent of grace and full of impatience would have a profound impact on making, marking, maturing, and multiplying disciples. Being patient is not idly waiting—it is bearing burdens, forgiving, serving, caring, and loving one another as we move toward being conformed into the image of God's Son.

"So then, as we have opportunity, let us do good to everyone, and especially to those who are of the household of faith."[97]

So in the goodness of God there is love, grace, mercy, and patience. As His disciples, we are the recipients of this character of God, and through our new nature we reflect the same toward others, and especially toward those in the Body of Christ (Galatians 5:22). Without the Fruit of the Spirit, the gifts of the Spirit are ineffective in the Body of Christ, and our witness in the world will be seen as perjury.

---

97. The Holy Bible: Galatians 6:10 (ESV)

The Revelation of God

(The Bible is the written revelation of Jesus, the Christ, who is the revelation of God. The Bible is a "Him" book. It is all about Him [Jesus, the Christ]. I have been hinting about this truth throughout these pages. Let me now focus specifically on Jesus the Christ, the supreme revelation of God.)

"God, who at various times and in various ways spoke in time past to the fathers by the prophets, has in these last days spoken to us by His Son, whom He has appointed heir of all things, through whom also He made the worlds; who being the brightness of His glory and the express image of His person, and upholding all things by the word of His power, when He had by Himself purged our sins, sat down at the right hand of the Majesty on high, having become so much better than the angels, as He has by inheritance obtained a more excellent name than they."[98]

In biblical history, there were various players who were consequential: Adam, the progenitor of the human race; Noah, the consequential hope of the continuum of the human race; Abraham, the father of faith; Isaac and Jacob, central figures of ancient and modern history; Moses, the emancipator of the people of God; Joshua, the captain of the Lord's army conquering the Land of Promise; David, the prototype of the coming of the Messianic King; Isaiah, Jeremiah, and Ezekiel, the prolific, audacious prophets of the Lord, and other pre- and post-exilic prophets who were consequential. But, Jesus Christ of Nazareth was the objective personage of redemptive history. The main purpose of Scripture is to point man to the person and purpose of Jesus, the carpenter's Son, and the Father's Son.

"You search the Scriptures, for in them you think you have eternal life; and these are they which testify of Me. But you are not willing to come to Me that you may have life."[99]

---

98. The Holy Bible: Hebrews 1:1-4 (NKJV)
99. The Holy Bible: John 5:39-40 (NKJV)

Philip found Nathanael and said to him, "We have found Him of whom Moses in the law, and also in the prophets, wrote—Jesus of Nazareth, the son of Joseph."[100]

The Bible is the exposition of Jesus. It exposes Him who is the self-disclosure of God. The prophets spoke for God, but Jesus Himself is God speaking. The Bible is a witness to the Witness of God; however, we dare not worship the Bible, but the God of the Bible, who is supremely revealed in Jesus Christ. You ask, why Jesus? He is the revelation of God. Creation declares the glory. The prophets proclaimed the glory of God. The Bible records His glory. But Jesus the Christ is the brightness of His glory. He is the final revelation of God.

"All Scripture is given by inspiration of God, and is profitable for doctrine, for reproof, for correction, for instruction in righteousness, that the man of God may be complete, thoroughly equipped for every good work."[101]

In the epistle to the Hebrews, we find Hebrew Christians threatening to go back to Judaic symbolism and animal sacrifices. They had come out of Judaism, but the pressures and persecution of the Jews—and perhaps their family members inside of Judaism—were causing them to look back. The writer of the epistle was encouraging and admonishing them not to go back. There was nothing to go back to because all was fulfilled in Jesus Christ—the final revelation of God. Their weakness in the faith made them vulnerable to go back, or to attempt to mix Judaism with Christianity. Listen to the writer as he refers to God: *"[He] has in these last days spoken to us by His Son"*[102]—suggesting that God has nothing else to say to us. He has spoken definitively and finally by His Son. Therefore, there is no need to go back or to look forward for a new revelation. If it is new, it is not true; and, if it is true, it is not new. God's final word is fixed in the Word that became flesh and lived in human history. God has no other message for mankind.

---

100. The Holy Bible: John 1:45 (NKJV)
101. The Holy Bible: 2 Timothy 3:16-17 (NKJV)
102. The Holy Bible: Hebrews 1:2 (NKJV)

Jesus is God's *"beloved Son . . . . Hear Him!"*[103] And the Bible, which is the testimony of Jesus Christ, both Old and New Testaments, demands that we embrace—unapologetically (*sola scriptura*)—the Bible alone. God has spoken by His Son, and the Bible is the literary witness of Jesus Christ who is the living Word of God. The Bible is the Word of God concerning the Word of God (John 1:1, 14; 1 John 1:1-4). As revelation, Jesus Christ is the full expression of God manifested in the flesh. In Colossians 1:15-19, He is viewed as the perfect personal imprint of God, predating above and beyond all creation. He is the precise exactness of God the Father. He is the perfect reproduction of Him, and yet He is distinct in person. Wow, what a mystery!

"Great indeed, we confess, is the mystery of godliness: He was manifested in the flesh, vindicated by the Spirit, seen by angels, proclaimed among the nations, believed on in the world, taken up in glory."[104]

Jesus is like the light of the sun. God the Father is the mass of the sun, and Jesus is the light of the sun. As we will discuss later, man, who was made in the image and likeness of God, serves as the moon created to reflect the light of the sun. Mankind is a copy (likeness versus is-ness), while Jesus is the exact representation of the very substance of God (John 14:9). Jesus is the light of the world because He is the Light. Glory has come among us through the humanity of Jesus. On the Mount of Transfiguration, the privileged three saw His glory (Luke 9:28-36), while others saw glimpses of His glory (Exodus 33:20-23) and signs of His glory (John 11:4). We cannot trust any other literary documents and books as witnesses to Jesus Christ, the Witness. There may be truth elsewhere and, if so, it must be measured by the proven text of Scripture. The hiddenness of God makes it impossible for man to discover Him. God must make Himself known to man. He must uncover Himself.

---

103. The Holy Bible: Matthew 17:5 (NKJV)
104. The Holy Bible: 1 Timothy 3:16 (ESV)

"Can you search out the deep things of God? Can you find out the limits of the Almighty? They are higher than heaven—what can you do? Deeper than Sheol—what can you know? Their measure is longer than the earth and broader than the sea."[105]

The mystery of God is manifested in and through the Incarnation (1 Timothy 3:16; 1 Peter 1:20). Old Testament manifestation was very much impersonal (Exodus 40:38). But, in Jesus, the glory of the Lord is personal. Listen to these profound words in the prologue of the gospel of John:

"And the Word became flesh and dwelt among us, and we beheld His glory, the glory as of the only begotten of the Father, full of grace and truth."[106]

Through the Incarnation, God is no longer symbolically with us; He is personally with us. As man, He pitches His tent among humanity and dwells personally with us. The transcendent God has come down to us; the remote God has come near to us. He is the exactness of God. He doesn't merely reflect God, He reveals Him exactly and perfectly. The writer of the epistle to the Hebrews declared, *"He is the radiance of the glory of God and the exact imprint of his nature, and he upholds the universe by the word of his power."*[107] As the Word made flesh, the man Jesus reveals God and can without contradiction declare to be the Son of God. He does not blaspheme the name of God by declaring equality with Him (Philippians 2:6-7). He is the Revelation of God. He is very God. Paul exclaimed that Jesus is *"the image of the invisible God, the firstborn of all creation."*[108] In Him the fullness of God dwells, Paul continues to exclaim. He existed before and beyond creation. Therefore, He preexisted and is preeminent, invading humanity from beyond it (Colossians 1:16-18). Jesus is not a mixture of God and man; He is fully God and fully man. However, God identifies Himself in

---

105. The Holy Bible: Job 11:7-9 (NKJV)
106. The Holy Bible: John 1:14 (NKJV)
107. The Holy Bible: Hebrews 1:3a (ESV)
108. The Holy Bible: Colossians 1:15 (ESV)

flesh. He becomes man by way of the Virgin Birth (Galatians 4:4-5) in order to reveal and to redeem. Even humans need bodies to distinguish themselves from each other. In Jesus Christ, God distinguishes Himself (John 14:8). To know the Father is to know the Son. To see the Father is to see the Son. The invisible and unknown God becomes visible and known supremely in and through Jesus Christ of Nazareth (John 1:18). Jesus Christ is the declarative witness of God cloaked in mystery (Revelation 1:4-6).

Jesus is the personification of glory that was temporally cloaked in humanity (John 17:5, 22). He never lost His glory. It was merely cloaked in emptying Himself (Philippians 2:7). However, He would not return to the "*Word in the beginning with God*" (see John 1:1; 8:58), but His glorifying reality will forever be as the God-man. The bodily resurrected Christ demands that His relationship with humanity continues throughout eternity as the God-man (Acts 1:10-11). As the first fruit of the Resurrection (1 Corinthians 15:20), He identifies His future with redeemed humanity. We shall have glorified bodies in association with His—glorified bodies to go with our glorified state (Romans 8:29-30).

Reflection

A disciple is an obedient follower of Christ, relating, reflecting, and reproducing disciples. This is our working definition of a disciple. Remember that I have postulated that Jesus did not *define* a disciple, He *described* a disciple. Yes! He is a learner and a student, but not in abstract and academic terms. What we see in Jesus' paradigm is an intimate relationship and transparent exposure of who He is and what disciples are to be, and a challenge to reproduce what was produced in them.

The grand and glorious purpose of humanity created in the image of God was to reflect His presence on the planet. God, the epitome of personhood, personalized creation with the creation of man

(Genesis 2:1-3), then He rested. Yes! The heavens are declarative in glorifying God but only impersonally, but man declares the glory of God in a personal way. God and man experienced Paradise until man became grown in God's house. Our primal parents reached for that which was not theirs to possess. They were dissatisfied with being created in the image of God and they wanted more. However, in their attempt to become more, they became less than what and who God purposed them to be. How tragic it was for mankind because the result was a life that would fall short of the glory of God (Romans 3:23). They had become slaves to sin and unrighteousness (Romans 6). Death and all that it brings entered their existence (Romans 5:12-14). They were not just separated from God—their God-given image had been severely stained (Isaiah 59:2; Romans 1:18-32).

The grace of God is seen in the fact that the image was severely stained but not removed. Mankind is not doomed to live or remain in the sub-human state that sin will take the sinner. In grace, God is still mindful of him and has purpose to care for him by visiting him (Psalm 8:4). He did not leave man nor remove man's capacity to respond in faith to His initiative of loving grace. Man, with his stained image, still possessed self-determination, self-consciousness, and moral consciousness. Humanity is a matter of image bearing even in its fallen state. Adam fell but did not lose his humanity in doing so. It was severely marred. His created purpose was damaged in the fall. The glory of God was dimmed and eclipsed by sin (Romans 3:23). The reflective light had vanished and man became darkness, walking in darkness and sitting in darkness (Ephesians 5:8). In sin, mankind became untruth in his darkened state. He loved darkness rather than light (John 3:19). The terribleness of sin is that it tells an untruth about God. Humanity was created to tell the truth about Him, which was and is the sole purpose of man on the planet. Everything else he does is ancillary to his existence. Ontologically, he is on earth to reflect the Father in heaven, being truth about Him.

The first Adam turned off the light thus plunging the world into darkness, but God sends Himself into the world (see John 1:1, 14) in the person of Jesus Christ, the second and last Adam, to turn the light back on in the world of darkness. Let me quote this lengthy but pivotal passage:

"There was a man sent from God, whose name was John. This man came for a witness, to bear witness of the Light, that all through him might believe. He was not that Light, but was sent to bear witness of that Light. That was the true Light which gives light to every man coming into the world. He was in the world, and the world was made through Him, and the world did not know Him. He came to His own, and His own did not receive Him. But as many as received Him, to them He gave the right to become children of God, to those who believe in His name: who were born, not of blood, nor of the will of the flesh, nor of the will of man, but of God."[109]

The power of Christ's presence in the darkness overcame it and exposed it for what it was—a contradiction of the God of Light. Not only did Christ expose darkness, but He also delivered those who would place their trust in God and operate redemptively through the cross of Christ (2 Corinthians 5:18-19). Those who received the Son became as John—witnesses of the Light. They experienced the transforming power of the light of the Gospel, bringing them out of the darkness and into the wonderful light (1 Thessalonians 5:4-5; 1 Peter 2:9). The only way back to our human ought-ness is through Jesus Christ, the Light of the world.

Although there is some Godlikeness in humanity, he will not return from his fallen state unless he falls at the nail-pierced feet of Jesus. As fallen, the glory of the Lord has departed from his humanity. He is in a state of "Ichabod"—the glory of the Lord has departed mankind (1 Samuel 4:21). Man cannot just decide to return. It will not happen through human achievements (John 1:13; Ephesians 2:8-10). The glory days of humanity will not return through the work of men, but through the work of Christ

---

[109] The Bible: John 1:6-13 (NKJV)

on that Old Rugged Cross. The glory is hindered by the gloom of sin. The sin of humanity must be atoned for and Jesus is the only one who is able to reconcile man back to his intended purpose (2 Corinthians 5:17-21). On Calvary, Jesus placed a spotlight on our sins by becoming sin for us. There, He made it possible for the stain on the image bearer to be removed.

Discipleship according to Jesus is more than a disciple's being a mere learner. He is a light bearer who shares the glory, light, and life of Jesus Christ. The gospel of John is full of this glorious truth concerning eternal life and marvelous light experienced by Jesus' disciples. Life and light are essential to Jesus and both are shared in the believing disciples (John 1:4; 3:16, 19-21, 36; 5:24; 6:40; 8:12; 17:1-5, 10, 22). We should see that there is a correlation between life, light, and glory. Through eternal life, we tell the truth about Christ (who is the life) and, therefore, we glorify God. This is reflective glory (1 Corinthians 6:19-20).

This restored image of God is only possible through Christ. The disciple reflects the image of God, namely through being conformed to the image of Christ (Romans 8:29). Through discipleship, the disciple is progressing from glory to glory (2 Corinthians 3:18). It is salvation that has to do with human recovery and not only the declared righteous status of the disciple known as justification. The working of sanctification is moving the disciple back to God's intended purpose for man. The Holy Spirit, who is actively working in the disciple through the Word of God, indwells the believer to glorify Christ (John 16:13-15; Romans 8:9-11). In the first Adam, the image is stained and deeply marred, and only through and in Christ is the image restored. This is the grand scheme of the Sovereign—to justify sinners in order to glorify saints (Romans 8:28-30). The humanity of the post-resurrected Christ guarantees salvation as human recovery. In the eschaton, the future, the disciple will be humanly like Jesus (1 John 3:1-3). The bodily resurrection of Jesus is the first fruit of human recovery in the future life. In Christ, we shall be a new humanity (2 Corinthians 5:17; 1 Corinthians 15:12-28, 35-58).

Presently, the disciple is called to reflect his Lord in his world. He is to be a reflection of Jesus Christ, influencing making a disciple for Christ where he lives, works, plays, and learns. Presence, not proclamation, is the reflective purpose of the disciple in his world. The moon influences the tides through its gravitational pull; however, its primary purpose is to shine light in darkness by reflecting the light of the sun. In the Sermon on the Mount, Jesus declared that His disciples were to just let their light shine and to realize that they were salt and light in a world of decay and darkness. It was being/existing as salt and light. Christ-like character was to be demonstrated in their concentric circle of influence. Disciples were to make music before including the lyrics. This is showing video before the audio; powerful silence before sound. *"But you shall receive power when the Holy Spirit has come upon you; and you shall be witnesses to Me in Jerusalem, and in all Judea and Samaria, and to the end of the earth."*[110] As witnesses, disciples are called to tell the truth about Jesus, who is the Truth, in the power of the Spirit of truth. Disciples live on the witness stand and are called out of darkness and then sent back into darkness to be witnesses of the Light. *"For you are all children of light, children of the day. We are not of the night or of the darkness."*[111] This verse speaks of who disciples are and not necessarily what they say. The disciples' state of being is in view here. Light is the nature of the disciple. In reflecting, the disciple is a witness in the world and a model for new believers in the discipleship process. He will influence new growth and maturity in the Body of Christ.

Jesus' disciples were new-birth disciples. They did not merely enroll in His school—they were born into His Father's kingdom. This may have been Nicodemus's plan, to merely enroll in a course with the Master Teacher, but Jesus confronted him with the demands of the kingdom of God.

Jesus answered and said to him, "'Most assuredly, I say to you, unless one is born again, he cannot see the kingdom of God.'" Nicodemus said to Him, "How can a man be born when he is old? Can he enter a second time into his mother's

---

110. The Holy Bible: Acts 1:8 (NKJV)

111. The Holy Bible: 1 Thessalonians 5:5 (ESV)

womb and be born?" Jesus answered, "Most assuredly, I say to you, unless one is born of water and the Spirit, he cannot enter the kingdom of God. That which is born of the flesh is flesh, and that which is born of the Spirit is spirit. Do not marvel that I said to you, 'You must be born again.' The wind blows where it wishes, and you hear the sound of it, but cannot tell where it comes from and where it goes. So is everyone who is born of the Spirit."[112]

Discipleship according to Jesus demanded the new-birth experience. All those who authentically followed Jesus, excluding Judas, obviously experienced the new birth. Surely Jesus' disciples heard His conversation with this Pharisee, who was a ruler of the Jews. They asked no questions about Jesus' conversation concerning the new-birth requirement for entering the kingdom of God because they had experienced the dynamic of the new birth themselves. These men were not mere followers of Jesus like the crowd we find in John 6 who gave up walking with Jesus after discovering the demands of discipleship (John 6:66). Jesus' disciples were not members of the fandom crowd. They had experienced inward transformation. Jesus reminded Peter and the rest of the disciples at the foot-washing encounter with Him that they had already been washed and only their feet needed washing (John 13:1-10). They had already experienced the washing of regeneration (Titus 3:5), but they only needed foot washing for holy walking.

If humanity is to recover from that tragic fall, then transformation must occur in order for the disciple to be conformed into the image of God's Son (Romans 8:29). The sinner must be changed; his or her life must be transformed. The mind, emotions, and will must be radicalized by the Gospel of Jesus Christ (Romans 1:16). Reformation is not it. Regeneration is the inward work of the Holy Spirit on and in the life of the sinner who submits to obeying the Gospel. It is a spiritual birth (John 3:6-8). It is not reforming the old but, rather, eradicating the old with the new (Romans 6: 1-14; Galatians 2:20). The old has been transformed into the new

---

112. The Holy Bible: John 3:3-8 (NKJV)

(2 Corinthians 5:17). It is not that something is added; rather, the old has become the new. Transformation has taken place in the life of the sinner. The old nature has been transformed into the new nature. The old nature—not the flesh—has been reborn. Adding a nature does not spell transformation and regeneration. The caterpillar is transformed into a butterfly; they do not co-exist. The caterpillar *becomes* the butterfly. The caterpillar and the butterfly do not co-exist at the same time. So it is with a disciple—the old and new nature do not co-exist. The essential essence of the new nature is the life of Christ in the disciple (Colossians 3:1-4; Galatians 2:20; 1 John 5:11-13). The old life has become the new life. The old man is dead in that it has been transformed into the new man.

Conforming presupposes that transformation has taken place in the life of the disciple. The disciple is able to conform because he or she has been transformed. Therefore, the disciple is being changed because transformation has taken place in the life of the disciple. He has been born again; therefore, authentic growth and maturity are possible. The disciple can be conformed into the image of God's Son because the life of God's Son is the life of the disciple (Romans 8:29). Glory is the hope of the believer because Christ is in the believer (Colossians 1:26-27). The disciple's destination is to be like Christ (1 John 3:1-3); therefore, he or she is presently conforming to His image, and he is confident that everything that will occur and has occurred in his or her life will lead to glorification (Romans 8:28-39). The ultimate goal is not only to be with Jesus, but also to be *like* Him.

Transformation Is in Continuum

Sanctification is taking place in the disciple's life. It is a process that began in regeneration and ends in glorification. The change has happened and is happening. Sanctification is salvation in continuum. The disciple has been saved and is being saved, and shall be saved—glorification. Listen to the apostle Paul:

I thank my God upon every remembrance of you, always in every prayer of mine making request for you all with joy, for your fellowship in the gospel from the first day until now, being confident of this very thing, that He who has begun a good work in you will complete it until the day of Jesus Christ; just as it is right for me to think this of you all, because I have you in my heart, inasmuch as both in my chains and in the defense and confirmation of the gospel, you all are partakers with me of grace.[113]

What a wonderful promise of guaranteed victory. However, in the meantime, there is a need for comprehensive discipleship—the maturing of the whole man. The disciple needs to grow spiritually and holistically. His mind, emotions, and will need to mature in the context of the spiritual. The disciple must know biblical truth about God in Christ and Christ in him. If transformation is to continue in the life of the disciple, growth in the grace and knowledge of the Lord and Savior Jesus Christ (2 Peter 3:18) must be experienced. This is cognitive and relational growth. Discipleship enables doctrinal stability but also devotional integrity. When grace growth precedes cognitive growth it balances the disciple. Grace growth will lead to a loving relationship with Jesus as Savior and Lord. Cheap grace is void of the Lordship of Christ. Grace growth led the apostle Paul to want *"to know [Christ] and the power of His resurrection, and the fellowship of His sufferings, being conformed to His death; in order that I may attain to the resurrection from the dead"* (Philippians 3:10-11, NASB). It did not lead him to embrace an easy beliefism and costless discipleship. Rather, it pushed him to be dissatisfied with mediocrity.

"Not that I have already attained, or am already perfected; but I press on, that I may lay hold of that for which Christ Jesus has also laid hold of me. Brethren, I do not count myself to have apprehended; but one thing I do, forgetting those things which are behind and reaching forward to those things which are ahead, I press toward the goal for the prize of the upward call of God in Christ Jesus."[114]

---

113. The Holy Bible: Philippians 1:3-7 (NKJV)
114. The Holy Bible: Philippians 3:12-14 (NKJV)

Grace growth gives disciples a desire to want to know Christ personally and intimately, rather than to just know about Him. Grace growth is healthy growth that enables healthy Body life. It thwarts legalism and self-righteousness in the Body of Christ (1 Peter 4:10-11; 1 Corinthians 15:10). Realizing the amazing-ness of abounding grace will not encourage a life of sin in the disciple because he or she has been birthed into the disciplines of the kingdom of God (John 3:3-5). The disciple lives under new management—the kingdom rule and reign of the King. Jesus is not only Savior, He is Lord (Romans 10:9) in the life of the disciple and of the life of the disciple. The disciple is no longer a slave to sin but to righteousness (Romans 6:15-23). The dynamic of the transformation is the spiritual reality of the death, burial, and resurrection of Jesus Christ (Romans 6:3-11). One does not merely decide to become a Christian disciple. It is not a matter of multiple choices, whereby one chooses Jesus over and against Mohammad or some other religious leader. It is a response to the work of the Holy Spirit in the life of the sinner. Not everyone responds to the wooing of the Spirit; and those who do not are subject to the sin of blasphemy against the Holy Spirit (Matthew 12:31-32). The Spirit woos through conviction of sins and righteousness and judgment, creating a deep sense of need and lost-ness. The sinner will never see the need of a Savior without the work of the Spirit. However, the work of the Spirit is not done without the work of the disciple in demonstrating and declaring the Gospel of grace (Romans 10:14-17). As seen in Ezekiel's vision of the restoration of Israel in Ezekiel 37, it takes the worker, the Word, and the Wind to transform dry bones into an army. The Holy Spirit operates through the Word of God and the worker (the disciple) to transform lives.

The reflective purpose of the disciple of Christ is found in presence. Proclamation will follow the disciple's presence. As salt and light are ontological in purpose, so is the disciple. The witness is video and then audio. It was the miracle performed in Lazarus that caused others to believe (John 12:9-11). Should not the miracle of the new birth performed by the Holy Spirit in the believer become the testimony of the disciple in the world's court? The message of good news is the miracle evidenced in the disciple. The message of hope and grace is displayed in the life of the disciple (1 Peter 3:14, 17). If Christianity is to be authentic and effective, then the Gospel must become flesh in the disciple of Christ. The Gospel is the power of God unto salvation (Romans 1:16) preached and, especially, demonstrated in the life of the disciple. Belief and behavior must have a symbiotic relationship to be used by the Holy Spirit to make and mature disciples. The disciple must model the miracle done in him or her in the power of the Holy Spirit (Acts 1:8). The Spirit of truth is essential to the disciple's telling the truth about Jesus, the Truth (John 14:15-17). The disciple must not only rightly divide the word of truth (2 Timothy 2:15; 1 Timothy 4:11-12) but also must not be straight and crooked, thus contradicting the Word of truth. To cut it straight while walking crooked can ruin the hearer and make the Gospel unbelievable.

The disciple has been entrusted with the glorious Gospel that shines through earthen vessels (2 Corinthians 4:7; 1 Timothy 1:11). The Gospel shines through weakness, not wickedness. Glory is reflected in the earthiness of the vessel. The vessel has been sharpened and formed by the Potter for the purpose of rendering Good News to the broken (Jeremiah 18:1-4). The light of the Gospel shines through the clay in order to demonstrate power in weakness. The behavior of the clay is in view more than the verbal pronouncement of the clay in 2 Corinthians 4:1-7. The privilege of being a steward of "this ministry" should affect the behavior of the clay. To attempt to take advantage of our clay-ness to operate in sinful behavior is not the point of the description. Sinful behavior will ruin the process of making and maturing disciples. In order for the lost to believe and for the saved infant to develop, the discipler must be a reflection of the glorious Gospel preached and explained. Therefore, human frailty is in view more than human failure. Although, in human failure, the discipler can be redemptive by demonstrating to the disciple how to handle failure, I do not believe that the description of the earthen vessel has failure in mind. The discipler can model for the disciple how to deal with failure. Moreover, it is important for the discipler to convey to the disciple that in human weakness God gets the glory. Reflection of the glory of God is seen best in the earthen vessel. The disciple needs to understand his or her utter dependency on the Holy Spirit. So, the disciple must persevere in prayer as a declaration of dependency. The life of a disciple is lived with a keen sense of being handicapped in order for God to get the glory. Living in the sphere of the supernatural demands that we realize our inabilities to accomplish our purpose without the Holy Spirit. When we are effective in the process of discipleship, the only explanation is the performance-enhancing Spirit. In weakness, the disciple can best give God the glory in the inexplicable. The apostle Paul gloried in infirmities (2 Corinthians 12:9) because power is manifested through weakness. What a paradox!

It is through relationships with sinners and saints that the reflective ministry of the disciple takes place. According to Jesus, the disciple is called to go into the world, His world, and make and mature disciples for Christ. Discipleship is not attending a class or taking a course; rather, it is doing life together with the saint and sharing life with the sinner. In the Word's becoming flesh, Jesus shared Himself with the world and made a life-changing investment in His disciples. He revealed the Father and modeled authentic humanity for His disciples to see (John 14:8; 1 Timothy 2:5-6). In reflecting, the discipler models becoming the example of conforming into the image of Jesus Christ (Romans 8:29). As pastors are examples to the flock (1 Peter 5:1-5), so is a discipler an example to his or her disciple. Discipleship best takes place in forming relationships, wherein the disciple can observe the life of the discipler as he or she conforms to the image of God's Son. The classroom setting can be a starting point, yet it must not be limited to the classroom but include the informal setting of doing life together in a relatable manner where there is mutual sharing of victories and defeats are experienced. Jesus' disciples walked with Him for three and half years. They learned and experienced much from being with Jesus. They heard and they saw Him as He moved them from being disciples to being apostles who would go and do the same as He had done to them.

The Fifth Thought: Reproducing Disciples

*"A Disciple is an Obedient Follower of Christ, relating, reflecting and **reproducing** Disciples"*

The God of the Bible is the God of reproduction. In Creation, He produced a universe out of nothing. He created with the intention to reproduce. The Sovereign is not stagnated. He created a world capable of development and growth. For the most part, all living things reproduce themselves. Without reproduction, extinction is inevitable. Continuity is a matter of reproduction, whether sexually or asexually. Not all animals reproduce sexually, but all humanity reproduces sexually. Mankind is commanded by the Creator to reproduce what He has produced—male and female.

Then God said, "Let us make man in our image, after our likeness. And let them have dominion over the fish of the sea and over the birds of the heavens and over the livestock and over all the earth and over every creeping thing that creeps on the earth." So God created man in his own image, in the image of God he created him; male and female he created them. And God blessed them. And God said to them, "Be fruitful and multiply and fill the earth and subdue it, and have dominion over the fish of the sea and over the birds of the heavens and over every living thing that moves on the earth."[115]

---

115. The Holy Bible: Genesis 1:26-28 (ESV)

The Creator did not add—He multiplied. He commanded the primal parents to partner with Him in propagating the earth through multiplication. Please note that we are dealing with the purposeful God. The spiritual finds significance in the natural. Many natural things in Scripture are illustrations for the spiritual. The fruitlessness of the fig tree in Mark 11:12-25 was primarily cursed because of its pretense, but its non-productivity was also in view. Disciples are saved to bear fruit. We are called not only to be productive but also to be reproductive.

Jesus' Analogy of Reproduction (John 15)

On His march to fulfill His ultimate purpose of securing human salvation, Jesus instructed His disciples illustratively:

"I am the true vine, and my Father is the vinedresser. Every branch in me that does not bear fruit he takes away, and every branch that does bear fruit he prunes, that it may bear more fruit. Already you are clean because of the word that I have spoken to you. Abide in me, and I in you. As the branch cannot bear fruit by itself, unless it abides in the vine, neither can you, unless you abide in me. I am the vine; you are the branches. Whoever abides in me and I in him, he it is that bears much fruit, for apart from me you can do nothing. If anyone does not abide in me he is thrown away like a branch and withers; and the branches are gathered, thrown into the fire, and burned."[116]

The One, who identifies Himself as deity in the "I Am" designation, teaches His disciples the phenomenal lesson of natural reproduction. The purposeful God has a higher truth He wishes to convey to His disciples: that everyone with Him is not of Him. Judas, who was fruitless, would not endure to the end but would experience the awful end of apostasy—being taken away from the presence of God. But Jesus encourages His true disciples who were already clean by the Word and in authentic relationship with the Vine that they will be reproductive and bear more and much fruit.

---
116. The Holy Bible: John 15:1-6 (ESV)

They will experience discipline when needed in order to grow. Although the discipline may be painful at times, it is not to destroy them but to develop them to bear more and much fruit (Hebrews 12:7-11). They must understand that without the relationship with the vine and the resource of the vine, they cannot accomplish their reproductive purpose in the world and church. All true disciples are fruit bearers by the nature of their relationship with the vine and their experience of the new birth, which is manifested in the Fruit of the Spirit (Galatians 5:22-23; Ephesians 5:9; Philippians 1:11; Colossians 1:10). Bearing fruit is a matter of good works done by the ones who are God's workmanship (Ephesians 2:10). Christian character spells fruit bearing. Therefore, disciples are pruned in order to become more like Jesus (Romans 8:29; 2 Corinthians 3:18). Moreover, what has been produced in the disciple is to be reproduced in others (2 Timothy 2:2).

I speak of generational discipleship. The most natural place for generational discipleship to happen is in the Christian home. Natural parents must see themselves as spiritual parents as well. As stated previously in this book, parents must not leave it to the church's children, youth, and young adult ministries to disciple their children. The family and the church must be engaged in a symbiotic relationship where the family is seen as the primary place to make a disciple. The church must become para-family in the discipleship process. The family is first base, and the church second base. A seamless connection between the home and the church should be developed when it comes to discipleship. Too much is lost where there is a gap between the home and the church when it comes to generational discipleship. Again, we see the purposeful God in instituting the family first as primary to society and even the church. He meant for the home to play the leading role in generational discipleship. It should not surprise us that families are under the attack of the enemy of God. The church needs disciple makers in the home if the church is to be whole and healthy. You cannot have a healthy congregation with sick families. Christian families must become the primary small groups of each congregation. Every husband and father must declare the sentiments of Joshua: *"But as for me and my house, we will serve the LORD."*[117] It might sound antithetical, but if we follow Satan we will discover where our emphases need to be placed. He is after men, marriages, and the family (Matthew 26:31). Satan, the world's system, and the flesh are opposed to married Christian men and seek to destroy their influence. Christian leaders lead with their character not credentials and charisma. Character fruit bearing is essential to the process of discipleship. The character produced by the Holy Spirit in the disciple maker is to be reproduced in the disciple through modeling.

Multiplication: The Most Effective Method of Church Growth

The last thing Jesus told His disciples was to go and make disciples of all nations. He did not tell them to go and evangelize. The method of evangelism would add to the church, but disciple-making would multiply members into the church. The more natural way of growing the church would be through relating, reflecting, and reproducing disciples. The fact that baptism followed the making of a disciple indicates that making a disciple was not the second step in salvation but, rather, the primary step. Marking the disciple through baptism declared the disciple's belongingness to Christ in salvation. We baptize believers (see Acts 2:38; 8:36-37). Evangelism is part of the multiplication process of relating, reflecting, and reproducing. In relating and reflecting, the video precedes the audio—the declaring of the Gospel. Being the Gospel greatly enhances hearing the Gospel. The preacher or witness that is sent with beautiful feet can enhance the message of the Gospel with an attractive lifestyle that precedes the verbal message (Romans 10:14-21). Jesus started with making disciples who became known as Christians (Acts 11:26). Somehow, we want to start with Christians who become disciples. A costless Christianity is one that does not begin with being a disciple of Christ. It is belief without obedience. Remember that our working definition of "disciple" is *an obedient follower*

---

117. The Holy Bible: Joshua 24:15 (ESV)

of Jesus, relating, reflecting, and reproducing disciples. Salvation commences with obeying the Gospel (Acts 6:7; Romans 1:5; 10:16-17; 16:26). There is always an element of obedience in faith. Dietrich Bonhoeffer stated, "Faith is only real when there is obedience, never without it, and faith only becomes faith in the act of obedience."[118] If there is no coexistence of faith and obedience, there is only nominal Christianity. Grace that frees the sinner from the results of sin is discipline grace that does not allow us to remain slaves of unrighteousness (Romans 6:17-18). The evidence of an authentic disciple is obedience.

The goal and purpose of Christian education (discipleship) is twofold: transformation by conforming to the image of Christ, and maturing to the level of spiritual parenthood. Through the discipleship process, the disciple is developing the Jesus nature, which is the new nature. In doing so, the disciple is enabled by the Holy Spirit within to maturate into spiritual parenthood. Listen to the apostle Paul as he described the task of disciple makers:

"[They] equip the saints [disciples] for the work of ministry, for building up the body of Christ, until we all attain to the unity of the faith and of the knowledge of the Son of God, to mature manhood, to the measure of the stature of the fullness of Christ, so that we may no longer be children, tossed to and fro by the waves and carried about by every wind of doctrine, by human cunning, by craftiness in deceitful schemes."[119]

The discipler assisted spiritual children to grow into spiritual adulthood. The discipler trains the disciple to stand against the schemes and tricks of the enemy, and to become a spiritual parent, building up the Body of Christ. Maturity leads to multiplication. Cognitive growth is never the destiny of Christian education; rather, it is to grow toward the image of Christ and become a vital participant in building up the Body of Christ through multiplication—reproduction. Being a disciple is not a spectator

---

118. Dietrich Bonhoeffer, *The Cost of Discipleship* (New York: Simon & Schuster Publishers, 1959), 64.
119. The Holy Bible: Ephesians 4:12-14 (ESV)

sport. You do not become a disciple to be in the audience but to be in the army, following Jesus in making disciples.

The Fruit of the Spirit (Galatians 5:22-23) is for reproduction, not for personal consumption. These character traits are the property of the new birth for the purpose of producing disciples and developing them to multiply. The manifestation of the fruit enables the discipler to plant and water the seed of the Gospel so that the Spirit of God can bring the increase—the making of a disciple (1 Corinthians 3:6). The farmer usually tills the ground before planting. He often mixes in fertilizer and nutrients to enrich the soil. Christian character prepares the ground of the sinner's heart to receive the Gospel. We dare not think we are actually the makers of disciples. The fruit bearer is a forerunner preparing the way of the Lord (Matthew 3:3). The discipler is part of the drama of transforming sinners into disciples of Jesus. Transformation is the work of the Spirit (John 3:5-8). Please note: If the new birth was necessary for Nicodemus to enter into the kingdom, then Jesus' disciples certainly had experienced regeneration (John 13:10-11). Jesus' disciples, unlike other disciples, were made disciples by entering into a dynamic relationship with Christ (John 17:20-26).

These nine qualities: *love, joy, peace, patience, kindness, goodness, faithfulness, gentleness, and self-control*—are the natural outgrowth of the transformed nature. They have to do with the new self in relationship with God and man. With God, there is the *love, joy, and peace* factor; with man, there is the *patience, kindness, and goodness* factor; and, with the self, there is the *faithfulness, gentleness, and self-control* factor. The first quality listed anchors the rest of the qualities. The disciples of Jesus are distinguished by *love* going upward and *love* going outward. They love God first in rank and preeminence, and then they love one another in the Body of Christ, overflowing into the world, to take notice and experience through missions and ministry (John 13:34-35).

God is glorified through multiplication (John 15:8). The Fruit of the Spirit are qualities produced by the Spirit. They are qualitative gifts that belong to the disciple through the gift of the Spirit (Romans 8:9). Our God is magnified through multiplication. He desires that what has been produced in the disciple be reproduced through the disciple. Trans-generational discipleship is Jesus' strategy for reaching the world with the Gospel. How can we reach the masses? With evangelism through discipleship as we go into our world relating, reflecting, and reproducing disciples. Evangelism is the disciple's sharing his or her Good News narrative. This is done in relationship with others by sharing both the video and the audio at home, at work, at school, and at play.

In the parable of the talents (Matthew 25:14-30), I believe Jesus taught the principle of multiplication as a strategy of discipleship when He commended making investments and He condemned nonproductive behavior. In discipleship, the disciple invests in others for the sake of salvation and sanctification. Talents are given to advance the kingdom enterprise in the world through multiplication. Jesus wants His disciples to be profitable. Unprofitable disciples are a contradiction to their purpose. Disciples are to pull their weight (talents) in making and maturing disciples. I shall not argue whether or not the man with the one talent was a false disciple who ended up eternally condemned; but he was slothful and unfaithful, which contradicted the nature of a true disciple of Jesus. Again, I must stress that the fruit of the Spirit is not for our benefit, but for God's glory and the edification of the Body of Christ. The making and maturing of a disciple is the most profitable thing we can do as Jesus' disciples. However, the church of disciples is so unprofitable by disobeying the last thing Jesus said: "*Go into your world and make disciples of the people in your concentric circle of influence.*"[120] The unfaithfulness of the disciple will not necessarily result in eternal judgment, unless the unfaithfulness is evidence of a follower being just a fan and not a follower of Christ—but we do know that the unfaithfulness of a true disciple can contribute to an unbeliever's being lost forever.

---

120. The Holy Bible: Matthew 28:19 (personal emphasis)

Discipleship and Social Justice

It is radical love that undergirds the other eight qualities of the Fruit of the Spirit, sending disciples into the world to make a difference for the ultimate purpose of making, marking, maturing, and multiplying disciples. Therefore, doing good in the social context through good works in confronting injustice and social ills is not simply engaging in social liberation but, moreover, salvific liberation. To undo the mess of the human fall, which is the cause of social ills, is to embrace the Christ of redemptive history, therefore not remaining in the romanticism of a paradise lost in Adam.

The two "great" biblical propositions—the Great Commission and the Great Commandment—may seem somewhat different, but not so. Driven by the Great Commandment, we must obey the Great Commission. In and through the Great Commission, disciples are aware of the root of the social ills—sin. Sin, in all its ugly forms, makes reconciliation with God essential to remedying and arresting man from the consequences of sin. Before there can be reconciliation between man and man, man must be reconciled to God (2 Corinthians 5:17-21). If we are to reach the masses, then disciples must become visible and vocal where there is injustice and social pain. But if making disciples is not the main focus, then the disciple's presence in the world is partial obedience. Why should the church do what others can do better and neglect what only the church can do? The church is best when she engages in discipleship. The question that arises in the church is, should the church engage in social ministries and teach a social gospel? If the church is missional, she is social. The church exists for the sake of the world. She is sent to do the business of the kingdom in the world. Jesus was social; therefore, His church must be social. The Gospel of Jesus Christ is not so much a social gospel but a salvific gospel for a society of sinners in need of a Savior.

Those who advocate a social gospel often quote Luke 4:18-19 to give credence to their social-gospel agenda. What was the good news to the socially poor, socially captured, blind, and socially oppressed? If we attempt to re-contextualize the passage, it can refer to a social agenda. However, I do not think correct contextualization renders the passage as social, but spiritual in nature. The metaphoric language of the passage speaks more to the spiritual plight and predicament of unsaved humanity. The mission and ministry of Jesus was an era of salvation—acceptable year of the Lord—Jubilee, the year of grace; the dawning of the day wherein it would please the Father to bruise the Son (Isaiah 53:10). Through Christ, the poor (bankrupted by sin), captured by Satan, blinded by untruth, and oppressed in sin would hear the Gospel of spiritual liberation declared by Him who would later become the personification of the Gospel declared. The pronouncement was that the spiritual healer had arrived. The initial disciples of Jesus were witnesses of this Good News. They were recipients of the Gospel and became Gospel carriers. As Jesus' disciples, we are proclaimers of this Gospel to the poor in spirit (Matthew 5:3). We also are recipients of this Gospel of grace, liberated to engage in comprehensive discipleship—therefore, effecting social change from the inside out. It is a spiritual salvation that gives voice to social ills without losing sight of man's greatest need—human redemption (Mark 8:36).

Matthew 25:35-40 is another passage of Scripture quoted by social gospel advocates to back up their social agenda. The timing of this passage depends on one's school of thought. There are eschatological differences. This passage raises such questions as, are the Gentile Christians ministering to the needs of believing Jews during the tribulation period? Is this passage referring to the Christians' responding to the human needs of marginalized people in society? Without debating the former question, the recipients of care in this passage are those related to the Lord. It is so intimate in that serving them is serving the Lord. They are members more than of the human race—they are members of the spiritual family of God. This is the focus of the passage; however, the people of the world must also be in the disciples' sight with a loving response to their needs without losing sight of their greater need (Galatians 6:10). Jesus had to constantly keep His disciples focused. It took them a while to understand and embrace the mission of the Master. It was actually on the other side of the Cross and the Resurrection that the light came on for them. *"So when they had come together, they asked him, 'Lord, will you at this time restore the kingdom to Israel?'"*[121] They were still fixed on Hebrew nationalism, and Jesus had to redirect them to the globalization of the gospel enterprise: *"But you will receive power when the Holy Spirit has come upon you, and you will be my witnesses in Jerusalem and in all Judea and Samaria, and to the end of the earth."*[122] The disciple of Jesus must focus on the last thing Jesus said, not letting it become the least thing he or she engages in—making, marking, maturing, and multiplying disciples.

Comprehensive discipleship in the sanctification process will deal with the disciple's conforming to the likeness of Christ. The changing of social policies that affect social injustice and racism is needed, but, at best, this is simply removing the spider web without killing the spider. Sin is the spider and the web of injustice, racism, etc, is the result of sin. In Matthew 28:20a, in the maturation process, there is the call for the disciple to obey what Christ had commanded, and in both testaments, the command to love God and others is the most fundamental of them all.

"Hear, O Israel: The LORD our God, the LORD is one. You shall love the LORD your God with all your heart and with all your soul and with all your might."[123]

And one of the scribes came up and heard them disputing with one another, seeing that he answered them well, asked him, "Which commandment is the most important of all?" Jesus answered, "The most important is 'Hear, O Israel: The Lord our God, the Lord is one. And you shall love the Lord your God with all your heart and with all your soul and with all your mind and with all your

---

121. The Holy Bible: Acts 1:6 (ESV)
122. The Holy Bible: Acts 1:8 (ESV)
123. The Holy Bible: Deuteronomy 6:4-5 (ESV)

strength.' The second is this: 'You shall love your neighbor as yourself.' There is no other commandment greater than these."[124]

The disciple is first challenged in Matthew 28:19-20 to prioritize making, marking, and maturing disciples, then to obey the command to love God and others. In loving others, the church can engage in speaking the truth in love against such social ills as injustice and racism.

Church and Discipleship

Included in making a disciple is multiplying a disciple. One disciple being the indirect cause of making another disciple is multiplication. To ensure reproduction, disciples are called to do life together in community. The church, the Christian community, is a macrocosm of the Body of Christ. For disciple *"to observe all things that [Christ has] commanded,"*[125] making practical the reality of *the baptism of the Holy Spirit* (1 Corinthians 12:13), is to become members of the visible church. The admonition in Hebrews 10 is crucial in experiencing reproduction:

"And let us consider one another in order to stir up love and good works, not forsaking the assembling of ourselves together, as is the manner of some, but exhorting one another, and so much the more as you see the Day approaching."[126]

This idea of a churchless Christianity is not Christ-like in principle or practice. Christ without a body is un-Christlike. The Groom without His Bride is incomplete. To have wheat, weak, and weed members in the visible church is always challenging and sometimes messy. This reality should not cause the disciple to abandon the visible church in search of that which does not exist—a functional church without any dysfunctional aspects. With weeds in the church (Judas), and the weak in the church (Peter), you will always have challenges. What the disciples need to know is whether or not

---

124. The Holy Bible: Mark 12:28-31 (ESV)
125. The Holy Bible: Matthew 28:20a (NKJV)
126. The Holy Bible: Hebrews 10:24-25 (NKJV)

Christ is in the church. If Christ is not in the church, then we might as well abandon it—because it is not His church. Another reason for abandoning the church is when it becomes our church and not His. It is His church not simply by name, but by nature and purpose (Matthew 16:13-20). The atmosphere for reproduction to happen in the visible church is the church becoming a grace place. I speak now of the grace endowments to serve one another and the grace disposition to love one another.

Spiritual gifts are given to each disciple. They are spiritual gifts because the Spirit gives them according to His will and purpose to whom He wills. As the Fruit of the Spirit is not personal, so the gifts of the Spirit are not private. The gifts are given for reproduction to take place in the Body of Christ. In Romans 12, you will notice an interesting sequence—a call not to conform, but to be transformed by the renewal of the mind (reproduction). Then, disciples are called to serve one another with their gifts and to behave as Christ's disciples in serving one another and others. Reproduction is the reason for the gifting of the disciple. In 1 Corinthians 12:7, there is the term "profit" that suggests increase. Edification is the goal of all spiritual gifts. Corporate and individual growth is reproductive growth. The gifts are given not for self, but for the sake of the whole (Romans 12:3; 1 Corinthians 12:7; 14:4-5). Self-edification is not the purpose of spiritual gifts. Gifts are given for creating a healthy Body of Christ. Misuse of the gifts is unhealthy for the Body. Gifts turned inward are unproductive. Gifts are produced by the Holy Spirit to assist disciples in making, marking, maturing, and multiplying disciples. Gifts are produced in the disciple but not necessarily for the disciple. They are not for private and personal use. Although there is joy in knowing you are gifted, they are not given for your sake but the sake of others in the Body of Christ. Dysfunction in the church at Corinth was due to several things, but one of the major things was the selfish use of their gifts, especially the gift of tongues. Because the Fruit of the Spirit wasn't manifested, the gifts of the Spirit were misused in the Corinthian church. The grace gifts were suffering because some thought they were superior to others, and others felt inferior (1 Corinthians 12:12-31). This was a very toxic environment for reproduction to take place in. The church was too messy for multiplication to be experienced in the life of the congregation. The saints in the Corinthian church were acting like "aints." This church wasn't a grace place; therefore, it was not a safe place for them to become who they were in Christ.

Healthy Body life creates an environment for experiencing reproduction. What is crucial for experiencing healthy Body life is grasping the reality of the one another-ness. In my book entitled *The Win*, I spent time and ink discussing the significance of the believer being baptized into the one another-ness. Realizing and relating to one another with this keen sense of an indispensable union places value on our mutuality in the Body of Christ. We are more than members of God's family. We are members of Christ's Body. In the Body, we are more than just interrelated (between); we are intra-related (within). A safe place for reproduction to happen is a grace place, which is a place where disciples have experienced grace and, therefore, can express and extend grace to one another. This is the grace disposition that is founded on loving one another. All the *"one another"* statements in the New Testament sit on the foundation of loving one another. Who would not feel safe in a congregation like that? Here are a few statements:

1. *"Be devoted to one another in brotherly love."* (Romans 12:10, NASB)

2. *"Honor one another above yourselves."* (Romans 12:10, NIV)

3. *"Live in harmony with one another."* (Romans 12:16, NIV)

4. *"Accept one another, then, just as Christ accepted you."* (Romans 15:7, NIV)

5. *"Serve one another humbly in love."* (Galatians 5:13b, NIV)

6. *"Carry each other's burdens."* (Galatians 6:2, NIV)

7. *"Be patient, bearing with one another in love."* (Ephesians 4:2, NIV)

8. *"Be kind and compassionate to one another."* (Ephesians 4:32, NIV)

9. *"Forgiving each other."* (Ephesians 4:32, NIV)

10. *"Submit to one another out of reverence for Christ."* (Ephesians 5:21, NIV)

11. *"Forgive whatever grievances you may have against one another"* (see Colossians 3:13).

12. *"Admonish one another."* (Colossians 3:16, NIV)

13. *"Spur one another on toward love and good deeds."* (Hebrews 10:24, NIV)

14. *"Live in harmony with one another."* (Romans 12:16a, NIV)

15. *"Love one another."* (John 13:34-35; 1 John 3:23; 4:7,11-12; 2 John 5, NIV); *"Love each other."* (John 15:12, 17, NIV)

16. *"Encourage one another daily."* (Hebrews 3:13, NIV)

17. *"Clothe yourselves with humility toward one another."* (1 Peter 5:5b, NIV)

The grace gifts and disposition manifested in the power of the Holy Spirit in the congregation will certainly enhance the making, marking, maturing, and multiplying of disciples.

The Final Thought:
Residential Presence in the Disciple

And Jesus came and spoke to them, saying, "All authority has been given to Me in heaven and on earth. Go therefore and make disciples of all the nations, baptizing them in the name of the Father and of the Son and of the Holy Spirit, teaching them to observe all things that I have commanded you; and lo, I am with you always, even to the end of the age."Amen.[127]

What kind of with-ness does Jesus speak of in these final words? His disciples had already experienced incarnational presence—God with them, the Word that was in the beginning with God, who was God, became man, and dwelt among them (Matthew 1:23; John 1:1, 14). This incarnate presence had become more intimate than any theophany and symbolic presence. God, in Jesus Christ, came in person to the planet. Not mere manifestations of God, but in human form, He came and dwelt among humanity. Then, He spent personal and intimate time with His disciples away from the many and the crowds, and He shared Himself with them and made them His disciples. As they walked with Him, they saw, they learned, and they experienced so many marvelous things. They had left all to follow Him, and His announcement of His departure greatly troubled them (John 13:36–14:6). But, He had to go to secure a permanent way to the Father through the cross and the empty tomb via the Resurrection. He had been temporarily with them for three and a half years, but promised a permanent presence that would only happen with His departure (John 14:15-18; 16:7).

---

127. The Holy Bible: Matthew 28:18-20 (NKJV)

He promised that He would never leave them: *"Lo! I am with you always, even to the climax of time. But yonder He goes into the sky, leaving them gazing"* (see Matthew 28:20; Acts 1:9-11). He has promised to return in the parousia (second coming of Christ), but what about in the present? It is through the Spirit of Christ that Christ is present. He is both with us and within us. He is omnipresent, but with specificity and exclusivity, He is present in His church and disciples members of the Body of Christ. No more intermittent presence (1 Samuel 16:14; 18:12; Psalm 51:11). He now remains with the disciple, and even in disobedience, He stays. Thank God He remains, though ineffective, in disobedience, but there still to restore the disobedient disciple. The disciples were troubled because Jesus would no longer be with them physically, but His going and sending the Holy Spirit would guarantee spiritual presence through the indwelling Spirit. he Spirit's presence is both comforting and evidential of their belonging-ness to Christ (Romans 8:9).

Because of the imperative to "make disciples," I think this with-ness speaks of effectual presence. Although He will never leave us, He is a permanent presence in the disciples, but His presence is only effectual in obedience. His power is more effective when we are not grieving Him. In the passage, the promise of His presence is connected to the purpose. His indwelling presence is unconditional, but now His effectual presence appears to be conditioned on obedience. As disciples engage in making, marking, maturing, and multiplying disciples, the Spirit's presence will manifest itself in power to obey. To accomplish Christ's vision and strategy for His church, disciples need power. God does not give disciples power. He gives them the Holy Spirit, who IS power. God does not share His power—He gives us the gift of the Spirit (Acts 2:38). The primary gift is the Holy Spirit, who gives gifts to every believer. Christianity is totally spiritual. It can operate in the flesh, but it is only effectual when it operates in the Spirit (John 15:26-27; Acts 1:8; Galatians 5:16-16). The enabling presence of the Spirit is vital to living an obedient life as followers of Christ. Obedience is evidential of the new birth and it distinguishes fans from followers. Evidence of salvation is not emotive behavior in the worship experience; rather, it is obedience in walking in the Spirit. In fact, walking in the Spirit enables obedience (Galatians 5:16-24). The disciples' relationship with Christ and one another is a matter of loving Him (John 14:15-31). To love like we have been loved by Christ requires the enabling presence of the Spirit. Followers of Christ are obedient not so much out of duty but out of devotion to Him.

The ability to relate to others is a beautiful human experience. Sharing life together is a good thing. The Creator said that it was not good for man to be alone (Genesis 2:18). When sin entered the human existence, relationships became challenging. Listen to these poignant words: *"To the woman he said, 'I will surely multiply your pain in childbearing; in pain you shall bring forth children. Your desire shall be contrary to your husband, but he shall rule over you.'"*[128] This was the situation on the horizontal level because there was significant trouble on the vertical level between God and man (Isaiah 59:2). Although reconciliation has happened through the atoning blood of Jesus (2 Corinthians 5:11-21), relationships need the performance-enhancing presence of the Holy Spirit. Even inside the reconciled community, relationships are difficult. We are created to relate to others, but because of the sin of selfishness and pride, we struggle to develop in the art of relating. Most of our human problems are relational in nature. We have difficulty relating, especially in marriage, and Christian marriages are not exempt. According to our working definition of "discipleship": "an obedient follower of Jesus, relating, reflecting and reproducing disciples," the Holy Spirit's presence is greatly needed in forming relationships toward making a disciple of Jesus Christ. The leading of the Spirit is necessary in the process of developing meaningful relationships. The relationship can happen outside salvation—making a disciple, and inside salvation—maturing a disciple. The discipler in both cases models the Christian life

---

128. The Holy Bible: Genesis 3:16 (ESV).

in a relatable and transparent manner. This dynamic encounter necessitates walking in the Holy Spirit. He must become the third Person in the discipleship process. Then, as the Spirit of truth, He is essential to the disciple's reflecting the image of Jesus. The disciple is to be a witness. He or she must tell the truth about the Truth (Jesus) in the power of the Truth (Holy Spirit).

Jesus said to him, "I am the way, the truth, and the life. No one comes to the Father except through Me."[129]

"And I will pray the Father, and He will give you another Helper, that He may abide with you forever—the Spirit of truth, whom the world cannot receive, because it neither sees Him nor know Him; but you know Him, for He dwells with you and will be in you."[130]

"But you shall receive power when the Holy Spirit has come upon you; and you shall be witnesses to Me in Jerusalem, and in all Judea and Samaria, and to the end of the earth."[131]

The Great Commission calls us to make disciples. This includes multiplying disciples. Making disciples through transformation is beyond the pay grade of the disciple maker, who does not actually transform the believer into Christ's disciple. The Holy Spirit is the source of this transformation. When I speak of a believer who is transformed into a disciple of Christ, I speak of no mere follower who is merely adhering to the teachings of a teacher—I speak of a radicalized follower who identifies with Christ through baptism as a response of an obedient faith. Discipleship according to Jesus demands transformation that is evident in conforming to the image of Christ. Disciple makers have an essential but limited role, but it is the Spirit who transforms the sinner into a disciple of Jesus (Romans 8:9-11). Again, let me pose this question: Would He have

---

129. The Holy Bible: John 14:6 (NKJV)
130. The Holy Bible: John 14:16-17 (NKJV)
131. The Holy Bible: Acts 1:8 (NKJV)

challenged Nicodemus with telling him he must be born again, had His disciples not experienced the new birth? I think not. His disciples also had been born of the Spirit (John 3:3-8).

The Afterthought: Discipleship According to Jesus

Now great multitudes went with Him. And He turned and said to them, "If anyone comes to Me and does not hate his father and mother, wife and children, brothers and sisters, yes, and his own life also, he cannot be My disciple. And whoever does not bear his cross and come after Me cannot be My disciple." (Luke 14:25-27, NKJV)

Discipleship according to Jesus demands radicalization. The strong language in the above passage is seemingly paradoxical to the nature of God, who is love. But it calls for us to get our priorities straight. The disciple of Jesus is measured by who is number-one in his or her life. Where is Jesus Christ in your life? This is the determinate question for the disciple. The primal question is, who takes precedence in your life? Who is the most important person in your life? Who is it that captures your mind, emotions, and will? Who is it that has all of you? Who is the peerless person that stands above everyone else in your life? Who is the "supreme being" in your world? The question is not whether you believe in a "supreme being"—it is more personal than that. Who is THE "supreme being" in your life? Who is in front of everyone else in your life? Whom do you seek to please more than anyone else? Who is your first love?

God is naturally first due to His preexistence. There is nothing and no one that precedes Him. He is before all that is. He is the first Cause. He cannot be guilty of pride because He is the "I Am that I Am." It is impossible and impractical for the Preeminent One to be arrogant and self-centered, because He is the self-existent One. It is unimaginable that the "I Am" God could be egotistical. God does not have to esteem Himself. He is already high and lifted up above everyone and everything. This is why He alone is worthy of worship—for He alone stands alone and is self-sufficient. He is ultimately independent. He is absolutely autonomous. He has the right to be in first place in our lives. He is the definitive, the First Person (Revelation 1:8, 17-18). He does not just speak in first person, He exists in first person.

He wants and demands first place in the human heart and life. God made man in His image and likeness to have a personal relationship with Him, not to be His equals. Adam and Eve were equals, but not God and man. God, who is Person, created persons in order to relate with Him. God is first person, angels are second persons, and man is third person. It wasn't because God was lonely that He created angels and man, for He was not lonely within His Trinitarian self. He was social and He created man in order to relate to him on earth. The relationship that our first parents had was thwarted and spoiled when they attempted to have equality with God. By believing Satan, who is the father of lies, they too became liars. Created to tell the truth about God through their humanity, they distorted that truth. Since sin had invaded the world through our first parents' failure, causing humanity at its best to fall short of God's glory, human salvation is necessary. The entire order of things is out of order because *"All we like sheep have gone astray; we have turned—every one—to his own way."*[132] Man thinks that he has come of age and so, therefore, he can act independently of the Creator. He has become full of himself, and God is no longer viewed as preeminent. The apostle explained it this way:

For although they knew God, they did not honor him as God or give thanks to him, but they became futile in their thinking, and their foolish hearts were darkened. Claiming to be wise, they became fools, and exchanged the glory of the immortal God for images resembling mortal man and birds and animals

---

132. The Holy Bible: Isaiah 53:6 (ESV)

and creeping things. Therefore God gave them up in the lusts of their hearts to impurity, to the dishonoring of their bodies among themselves, because they exchanged the truth about God for a lie and worshiped and served the creature rather than the Creator, who is blessed forever! Amen.[133]

Not only is God not viewed as preeminent, He has also been reduced to the level of mortal man and creatures. He occupies no prominent place in the heart and life of the unbeliever. Honorable mention is about the best an unbeliever gives to God. The unbeliever is not necessarily a nonbeliever. The unbeliever lacks faith in God, but the nonbeliever denies the existence of God. He has no faith in God. There is no room for God at all in the life of an atheist, and there is no particular or personal place for God in the life of an agnostic and unbeliever. But, sadly, in the life of some believers, God is not in first place. Faith that places God in first place is a faith that cannot be separated from discipleship. Cognitive faith that does not bring about transformation and the newness of life is not saving faith. The Gospel received by grace through faith *is the power of God unto salvation* (Romans 1:16). It saves from the penalty and power of sin but not the presence of sin (Romans 6:17-18; 1 John 1:8-10).

Many Bible interpreters and Christians struggle with the demands found in the Lukan text (Luke 14:25-27) because it appears to suggest a meritorious salvation. Faith does not appear to be alone in salvation. Therefore, the text must refer to a post-salvation demand and experience. To understand Jesus' teaching in this passage is crucial. Not to understand and respond to the demands of this passage may result in falling short of an authentic relationship with Christ. To make discipleship a post-salvation experience is to suggest that Jesus was teaching the crowd about discipleship when they needed salvation. Why challenge them to engage in post-salvation when they had not believed in Him? If discipleship is cross-bearing and salvation is coming to the cross, as some believe, then why would Jesus challenge them with this hard demand and they were

---

133. The Holy Bible: Romans 1:21-25 (ESV)

unbelievers? If salvation is not synonymous with discipleship, then why did Jesus run the Rich Young Ruler away from an opportunity to experience eternal life with His discipleship demands?

Think with me: Is it possible that discipleship is optional in Christianity? Is it possible to be a Christian and not a disciple? You can believe in Jesus, but not live a life of obedience. You can come to Jesus by faith, but not follow Him in obedience. You can be delivered from the penalty of sin, but practice sin as a lifestyle. You can have belief without behavior. He can be your Savior, but not your Lord. Bonhoeffer said, *"Cheap grace is the deadly enemy of our church."*[134] Is it that we desire to enter heaven without being born into the discipline of the kingdom of God? The demand placed on Nicodemus was that he must be born again (John 3:5-7). The demands of the kingdom are tantamount to the demands of discipleship. Jim Wallis stated, "The response of faith always embraces the call to discipleship, the call to show forth the reality of the new life and freedom by following in obedience to Christ. The call to faith and to discipleship are the same and cannot be separated."[135]

Why would Jesus be so demanding of Nicodemus and the Rich Young Ruler and simply call us to mere cognitive faith in Him? The demons have cognitive belief in the existence of God. Satan is not an atheist or an agnostic; he believes that the Gospel is true, but he and his friends are eternally lost (James 2:19). Therefore, believing and receiving the Gospel message is much more than intellectual assent. It is shifting one's allegiance to Christ as Lord (Romans 10:9). It is denouncing the old allegiance in favor of the new (2 Corinthians 5:17). It is dying to the old and living in the new (Galatians 2:20). It is not merely accepting Christ; rather, it is surrendering to Him as Savior and Lord. When the disciples heard the demands of discipleship presented to the Rich Young Ruler, they asked, *"Who then can be saved?"*[136] The short answer is that *no one* can be saved

---

134. Bonhoeffer, *The Cost of Discipleship*, 47.
135. Jim Wallis, *Agenda for Biblical People*, 26.
136. Matthew 19:25b (ESV)

without the move of God upon the life of the sinner. It appeared impossible to them. But, the enabling gift of faith (Ephesians 2:8) has within it more than a cognitive response to the Gospel—it has a transforming power in it (Romans 1:16). It transforms the old nature into the new nature.

When this dynamic of the Holy Spirit happens in the believer's heart, it produces only one kind of Christian—a spiritual Christian. There is no such thing as a carnal Christian. A carnal Christian is antithetical or incompatible to the Christian's new nature. There are two types of persons in the world: the natural and the spiritual. By spiritual, I mean those who are born of the Spirit (John 3:6-8), baptized and indwelled by the Spirit (1 Corinthians 12:13). The notion that there are carnal and spiritual Christians is unbiblical and undermines the effectiveness of the church's witness in the world. There is carnal behavior, but not carnal Christians. Christians can act carnally, which is acting unlike who they are—spiritual. To be Christian is to be spiritual, and to be spiritual is to be Christian.

The First Person

God is objectively the First Person. In the disciple, He is both objectively and subjectively the First Person. He is subjectively the First Person in the disciples, in that He is often not practically first. As stated previously, He is first person by virtue of His pre-existence and self-existence and, I add, His transcendence. We cannot make Him first. He is objectively first without our permission and acknowledgment. He is first, regardless of any pronouncement on our part.

The Significance of Coming to Him

"If anyone comes to me and does not hate his own father and mother and wife and children and brothers and sisters, yes, and even his own life, he cannot be my disciple." (Luke 14:26, ESV)

Jesus' appeal to the crowd to come to Him was salvific in nature. They had been coming for superficial reasons. They were not interested in spiritual things. They came to see miracles, to receive temporal bread, and to hear words of social revolution and restoration of the Davidic kingdom. Jesus' call for them to come demanded more than an emotionally driven, superficial, self-seeking, temporary response of transient followers (John 6:26). He was not calling for fans, but for authentic followers. *"Come to Me."* Not to the church or to a cause, but to Christ. Come to the person. You can join a church and miss Christ. You can embrace a noble cause and fall short of knowing Christ. There are many churchgoers, but few Christ followers. Nominal Christians (in name only) go to church, but authentic Christians are on the go for Christ. It is a salvation call to come to Him. It was not a mere call to come. It is a call unto the restless. *"Come to me, all who labor and are heavy laden, and I will give you rest. Take my yoke upon you, and learn from me, for I am gentle and lowly in heart, and you will find rest for your souls. For my yoke is easy, and my burden is light."*[137] It was a call for those who knew they were in need of rest because of the drawing power of God in salvation (John 6:44). So they could come because He (Jesus) came to them. We come to Jesus because He took the initiative and came in redemption to us. God is definitely the main character and player in our redemptive experience. If we come to Him, it is because He first came to us. We have responded to God's predetermined plan to bring us unto Himself through the blood of His cross (Colossians 1:20). You cannot truly come to Him and remain the same. If you come in faith, you will leave healed. If you come in faith, and not with flattery, you will leave born again. If you come in faith, and not full of self, you will receive eternal life. If you come in faith, you receive the Bread of Life and everlasting water. If you come in faith, His grace and peace are yours. If you come in faith, His joy and contentment are yours. If you come in faith, His forgiveness and reconciliation are yours. If you come in faith, His righteousness is yours,

---

137. The Holy Bible: Matthew 11:28-30 (ESV)

and your sins are His. The marvelous thing about coming to Jesus is that you come as you are, but you won't remain as you are after coming.

The Significance of Our New Relationship

We are called to come into a new relationship with Christ wherein He becomes the preeminent person in our lives. The language used to describe this new relationship is so strong that without interpretation it seems to be obscene and absurd. How dare the God of love speak of hate as something positive? It is unimaginable that He would command us to hate our parents, spouse, children, siblings, and even ourselves. This hate language coming from God is almost unbearable to the ears. Who would want to be the disciples of Jesus Christ if it demands hate towards those who are normally the focus of our love? If He commanded me to hate my enemies, I might agree with that, but my loved ones? That is too much to ask in order to follow Him. The difficult sayings of Jesus—like "eating and drinking His blood," "putting to death the flesh," and "turning the other cheek," and other sayings—are not as stinging as hating your loved ones. What is the meaning of this disturbing demand?

Our love for God is so supreme and superior that relational love toward everyone else seems to be the opposite of love. For the disciple of Christ, to love God is to love others less than Him. Our love for God is preferred above and before parents, spouse, children, siblings, and self. The meaning of hate in this passage, Luke 14:26, is not having a strong aversion against someone, but having a love for God that out-distances all other love relationships. Scripture commands us not to hate, but for husbands to love their wives as Christ loved the church; for wives to lovingly respect their husbands; for children to lovingly obey their parents; for parents to lovingly discipline their children; for believers to love one another as Christ has loved us; and for believers to love their enemies (Romans 12:9-21). So, to hate is antithetical to who we are as disciples (1 John 3:11-18), but if Christ is not our first love, then we are not His disciples. The exaggerated contrast is illustrated in Jacob's relationships with Rachel and Leah (Genesis 29:30-31). Jacob loved Rachel more than Leah. So hate in this context means to love less. The church in Ephesus was said to have *"left [their] first love."*[138] The love they had at first was struggling for preeminence. Their work had overshadowed their walk with Christ.

The Significance of Prioritizing

Jesus is calling for His disciples to live a prioritized life. As the Lord informed Israel not to have any other gods before Him, we must not place our loved ones in the place reserved for God. We do them an injustice by putting them in that holy place. Our God is a jealous God. He will not tolerate the sin of adultery. We have no open-ended relationship with Him. We love others, but not like we love Him. The love relationship between a husband and wife is supposed to be the paragon of God's love relationship with His people, and Christ's relationship with His church. It is to be exclusively monogamous. Church leaders are to be examples to the members of a monogamous marriage of a man and a woman (1 Timothy 3:2, 12). First place is the place of worship and adoration. To place your loved ones in that spot is to place them in opposition to the true God. What does it look like practically for God to be in first place? The disciples lived to please God above all others, and they lived to serve God above all others. Their total being was committed to Christ (Mark 12:30).

The priority position is vividly understood when allegiance to Him is much deeper than family ties (Matthew 10:34-39). Christ supersedes, precedes, and takes precedence over family. Jesus operated from the primacy of the eternal family over the earthly family when it came to doing the Father's will (Matthew 12:46-50). The will of the Father supersedes whims of family. The business of the Father is more important to the disciple than family business (Luke 2:49). Moreover, family business should be contextualized in the Father's business—making, marking, maturing,

---

138. The Holy Bible: Revelation 2:4 (ESV)

and multiplying disciples—the family becoming the primary place in discipleship.

The Significance of the Cross in the Life of Disciples

The importance of the Cross in salvation is obvious throughout Scripture. The cross of the Christ of Calvary without a doubt is the poignant place of human history. It is the place where the holy God intersects with sinful man. There, He was at work reconciling man back unto Himself (2 Corinthians 5:18-19). Calvary was the designated place to atone for sins, purchase human redemption, and offer ultimate forgiveness. Jesus was King, but we desperately needed a Savior. With His cross and not His scepter He justified us, freeing us from condemnation (Romans 8:1). So, we are to glory in His cross. That woeful place that caused some to stumble and others to cry has become a wonderful place for believers (1 Corinthians 1:23-25).

Inside of salvation there is the cross of service, submission, and sacrifice. Dr. Luke's gospel is not a journal, but a gospel treatise written backwards from the resurrection. Although Jesus mentioned the Cross before He bore and hung on the cross, He knew His disciples would have their crosses. The life of the cross would become their experience as His disciples (Matthew 10:16-25). The Cross was not Jesus' experience—it would be the experience of every disciple of Jesus from regeneration to glorification. We share in Christ's crucifixion. He died for our sins, and we have died to our sins. The cross of death has become life for the disciples of Jesus (Philippians 1:21; Galatians 2:20; Romans 6:2-6). There is life through His death, and there is life when we participate in His death. *"When Christ calls a man He bids him come and die."*[139] Is this why so few men come to Him? You give Him your life, and He gives you His life. The call to come to Him is not only a call to love our families less, but also ourselves. It is a call to come to the end yourself (Luke 9:23, 24). Bonhoeffer states, *"It is that dying of the*

---

139. Dietrich Bonhoeffer, *The Cost of Discipleship*, 89.

old man which is the result of his encounter with Christ. As we embark upon discipleship we surrender ourselves to Christ in union with his death—we give over our lives to death."[140] The disciple's testimony in physical baptism is a statement of willingness to share in Jesus' death in salvation and service.

Self-hate is not the point in Luke 14:26. We are not necessarily called to loathe ourselves. After all, we are created in the image and likeness of God. He made us a little lower than angels (Psalm 8:4). Of all creation, man reflects His being more than all. There is a place for constructive pride and self-worth and self-love, if contextualized in Christ-esteem (1 Corinthians 15:10; Ephesians 1:3-14). If there is any self-esteem, it originates in the fact that God has esteemed humanity in that He created man with distinction, giving him dominion over the works of His hands. But, moreover, man is esteemed, in that God became man, died in the place of man, and Jesus' resurrection as the first fruit of complete human recovery (1 Corinthians 15:12-23, 35-58). Bodily resurrection is related to the disciple's glorification, which is the final act of our salvation journey.

It is humanistic self-esteem that is troubling to the purpose of God: when man does not realize and function with the sense that he is who he is because God willed it so; when man becomes full of himself, thinking that he has become grown in God's house, foolishly seeking autonomy from the God upon whom he is utterly dependent. The prophet Isaiah describes it this way: *"We all like sheep have gone astray; we have turned—everyone—to his own way."*[141] We are prone to think more highly of ourselves than we ought. There is the itch in the human psyche to have more and be more than we were created to have and to be. Man was not and is not satisfied with stewardship, he seeks ownership. He is not happy with being created in the image of God, he wants God's spot. This is why first place must be ascribed to God alone. God will have no other god before Him, not even human gods. This god complex is what drove Adam and Eve out of the

---

140. Ibid., 89.
141. The Holy Bible: Isaiah 53:6a (ESV)

Garden of Eden. It is the desire for human independence, which is utterly impossible, "*In [God] we live and have our being*" (Acts 17:28). Humanity rebels against God, who gives them their existence and sustenance. How foolish it is for dependent children to attempt to be independent while they are utterly dependent.

The demand placed on the disciple is to love God more than self. It is not a call not to love self. Self-hate is meaningless and unhealthy, but narcissism is also unhealthy. There is a self-love that is unhealthy, and there is a self-hate that is equally unhealthy. Too much self or too little self can be a serious problem. Self-centeredness is life turned inward, not upward or outward. It is self-glorification, which is a form of idolatry. This is the self-love that the apostle Paul spoke against in 2 Timothy 3:2. To have balance between too little self and too much self, Christ must be in first place in our lives. We worship God because He is worthy, but we also worship to remind ourselves of who we are when not in relationship to Him. Worship helps us to have the right perspective. He is Creator and we are creatures.

The doctrine of total depravity does not convey that man is totally worthless and devoid of any good or good deeds. It is not my aim to explore this teaching in-depth, but to simply point out that man is not as bad as he can be, and that his self-worth is not removed because he is totally depraved. God does not create worthless things. By total depravity, we mean that man is incapable and totally disabled in making himself right with God. Even in his acts of doing good, with impure motives, his heart reveals he is desperately wicked and, therefore, disabled within himself to please God (Jeremiah 17:9-10). To find and operate in our true selves, we need to lose ourselves. What a contradiction. Self-denial and self-abnegation are crucial to being Christ's disciple. It is a call to radicalization. It is a call to surrender self to another person, not just to an ideology. Jesus summons us to embrace His radical kingdom and righteousness (Matthew 6:33) and join Him in living life beyond the norm. He demands that His followers be poor in spirit, mourn over sins, demonstrate strength in weakness, have an insatiable desire for righteousness, show mercy, be peacemakers, be pure in heart, rejoice when persecuted, influence the earth and world as salt and light, practice righteousness, be angry and sin not, live a lust-free life, stay married, let our words be consistent, don't be revengeful, love our enemies, give to the needy, be people of prayer, fast to know Him intimately, be good stewards of money and possessions, and be free of worry (Matthew 5:1-6:34). The radical demands make dying to oneself necessary by experiencing a radical change—regeneration. Radicalization of the Christian is more dynamic than radical Islam. It involves an inward transformation, not merely an ideological one. This change is new life, not merely a new way of life. Christ's life is the very essence of the transformed life in the disciple (1 John 5:11-12).

The new life in the disciple is characterized by loving oneself less and loving God more. Jesus pleased the Father supremely in taking up His cross (Romans 15:3; Isaiah 53:10; Philippians 2:8). Therefore, His disciples must also please God through the Cross. To take up the cross is to major in what Christ majored in. The life of cross bearing is to engage in the ministry of reconciliation (2 Corinthians 5:18-21). The life of cross bearing is focused on Christ and Him crucified (1 Corinthians 2:2). It is denying self for the sake of the Gospel of the cross. To love oneself less for the sake of fulfilling the purpose of the Cross is the business of the disciple of Jesus. Disciples are called to come to the end of themselves like Paul said Jesus did (Philippians 2:7-8). The essence of cross bearing is living a surrendered life of sacrificing to accomplish God's will. After we come to Jesus, we must come after Him in ministry and the Gospel of reconciliation.

The Significance of Complete Christianity

To enter Christianity from the wide gate is dangerous because of its deceptive nature. It is nominal Christianity wherein the person is a Christian in name without experiencing a new nature. It is incomplete Christianity when one simply makes a decision for Christ without a conversion experience. When people come to church without coming to Christ it is incomplete Christianity. Really, incomplete Christianity is not being a Christian, but thinking you are because you are a member of the church and you have been baptized—thinking the act of baptism makes you a Christian. o enter by way of the wide gate is superficial; it is where the seed of the Gospel did not fall on productive ground, but on nonproductive ground (Mark 4:3-9). A Christianity that demands nothing produces nothing and is not of Christ. In Luke 14:25-27, Jesus is addressing his disciples with the crowd listening in on the teaching. This was a crowd of would-be disciples. To be true followers of Christ they must enter the narrow gate of discipleship (Matthew 7:13-14). Costless Christianity is incomplete Christianity. Just like salvation cost Jesus His life, a response to the Gospel of grace is a faith that calls for you to surrender your life to Jesus' Lordship (Romans 10:9). That placed the first responder to His lordship in grave danger when declaring that Jesus was Lord.

The demand of Jesus to the crowd that overheard His teachings was for them to become His disciples. He did not call them to belief, but to obedience and to follow Him after coming to Him. The men who became the first disciples were called to renounce all, divorce all relationships, and give away all their possessions and follow Him. They were to divorce everything and devote themselves totally to Him. Christ demanded that He would be in first place in their lives. The call to discipleship was at the very beginning of their Christianity. It did not come after salvation. It was intertwined in their salvation experience. Their faith was seen in their response to the call to drop their nets and follow Jesus. What have you given up to follow Jesus? Who or what is no longer in first place that Christ might be in first place? What have you renounced in order that you might receive Christ? For Christ to be in first place, you must see knowing Him as a surpassing value (Philippians 3:8). He is the Pearl of Great Price that you are willing to renounce everything to have Him (Matthew 13:45-46).

If you have not suffered loss, your Christianity is probably incomplete. You should have suffered the loss of worldly pleasures, friendships, relationships, positions, prestige, power, and prominence. What was once valuable to you has lost its prominence in your life. It is not necessarily sinful, meaningless, and negative things that have become loss for Christ, but valuable, profitable, and good things. The higher the worth of those things you have counted as loss for Christ, the more the surpassing value of Christ has become. Christ has beat out all top contenders for the place of prominence in your life. Although first place is a way of life for the disciple, contenders always challenge it. Discipleship is the process of making the objective truth, and the subjective a reality in the life of the disciple.

The Final Afterthought:
This Is Discipleship According to Jesus

To effect ministry in the twenty-first century, we must fulfill the strategy of the first-century ministry according to Jesus (see Matthew 28:19-20).

Remember—
"And I am sure of this, that he who began a good work in you will bring it to completion at the day of Jesus Christ."[142]

---

142. The Holy Bible: Philippians 1:6 (ESV)

Bibliography

Anderson, Ray S. *On Being Human: Essays in Theological Anthropology.* Grand Rapids, MI: Wm. B. Eerdmans Publishing Co., 1982.

Arn, Win, and Charles Arn. *The Master's Plan for Making Disciples.* Pasadena, CO: Church Growth Press, 1982.

Barna, George. *Growing True Disciples.* Colorado Springs, CO: Waterbrook Press, 2001.

Bennett, Ron. *Intentional Disciple Making.* Colorado Springs, CO: Tyndale House Publisher, Inc., 2001.

Bonhoeffer, Dietrich. *The Cost of Discipleship.* New York: Simon & Schuster Publishers, 1959.

Briscoe, Stuart. *Discipleship for Ordinary People.* Wheaton, IL: Harold Shaw Publishers, 1988.

Campbell, Fred. *The Win: Knowing and Pursuing Our Education.* Nashville, TN: Townsend Press, 2017.

Chan, Francis. *Multiply, disciples making disciples.* Colorado Springs, CO: David C. Cook Publishers, 2012.

Chandler, Matt. *The People of God.* Nashville, TN: B&H Publishing Group, 2014.

Cosgrove, Jr., Francis M. *Essentials of Discipleship.* Colorado Springs, CO: NavPress, 1980.

Costas, Orlando E. *The Church and Its Mission: A Shattering Critique from the Third World.* Wheaton, Illinois: Tyndale House Publishers, 1974.

DeYoung, Kevin, and Greg Gilbert. *What Is the Mission of the Church?* Wheaton, IL: Crossway, 2011.

Erickson, Millard J. *Christian Theology*, 2nd Edition. Grand Rapids, Michigan: Baker Publishing Group, 1998.

Evans, Tony. *Kingdom Disciples*. Chicago: Moody Publishers, 2017.

Fletcher, Jesse C. *Practical Discipleship*. Nashville, TN: Broadman Press, 1980.

Gallaty, Robby. *Growing Up*. Nashville, TN: B&H Publishing Group, 2013.

———. *Rediscovering Discipleship: Making Jesus' Final Words Our First Work*. Grand Rapids, MI: Zondervan, 2015.

Geiger Eric, Michael Kelly, and Philip Nation. *Transformational Discipleship*. Nashville, TN: B&H Publishing Group, 2012.

Hanks, Jr., Billie, and William A. Shell, (edited). *Discipleship*. Grand Rapids, MI: Zondervan Publishing House, 1981

Henrichsen, Walter A. *Disciples Are Made Not Born*. Colorado Springs, CO: David C. Cook Publishers, 1974, 1988, 2018.

Horton, Michael. *The Gospel Commission*. Grand Rapids, MI: Baker Books, 2011.

Hull, Bill. *The Disciple-Making Pastor*. Grand Rapids, MI: Fleming H. Revell Company, 1988.

Iorg, Jeff. *The Character of Leadership*. Nashville, TN: B&H Publishing Group, 2007.

MacArthur, John. *Evangelism: How to Share the Gospel Faithfully*. Nashville, TN: Thomas Nelson, 2011.

—————. *The Gospel According to Jesus.* Grand Rapids, Michigan: Zondervan Publishing House, 1988.

Phillips, Keith W. *The Making of a Disciple.* Los Angeles: World Impact Press, 1981.

Putman, Jim. *Real-life Discipleship.* Colorado, Springs, CO: NavPress, 2010.

Sproul, R. C. *Essential Truths of the Christian Faith.* Carol Stream, IL: Tyndale Publishers, Inc., 1992.

Toplady, Augustus M., 1740–1778. "Rock of Ages, Cleft for Me," in *United Methodist Hymnal,* Hymn #361. Nashville, TN: The United Methodist Publishing House, 1989.

Wallis, Jim. *Agenda for Biblical People.* New York: Harper & Row Publishers, 1976.

Warren, Rick. *The Purpose Driven Church.* Grand Rapids, MI: Zondervan, 1995.

ABOUT THE AUTHOR

Pastor Fred Campbell

Pastor Fred Campbell has served as Mt. Zion Baptist Church's pastor for more than forty years, being one of the longest-tenured pastors in the San Francisco Bay Area. His innovative and proven leadership has left an indelible mark, leading people towards spiritual maturity. Over the span of his Gospel ministry, he has been a champion for discipleship, faith at home, education, empowering men, and more. Members enjoy his biblically sound preaching and teaching, humor, and personable demeanor. He is currently leading Mt. Zion in pursuing the win, where each member grows in relationship with Jesus and into maturity in the body of Christ.

Pastor Campbell is one of our nation's trailblazing leaders, serving in various capacities throughout his ministry. He has served in the California State Baptist Convention, Inc., in various leadership positions, including Financial Secretary, Director of Christian Education, and Congress of Christian Education President. In 2002, under the mantra of "Building Healthy Churches," he became president of the California State Baptist Convention, guiding it in becoming a viable resource to local churches. Borne out of his service to our state convention, Pastor Campbell is also a leader in the National Baptist Convention, USA, Inc. He served under the Shaw administration as historian, at-large board member under the Scruggs administration, and Chairman of the Board under the Young Administration.

Pastor Campbell has a deep passion for pastors, ministers, and their wives and provides wise counsel and support to pastors throughout the nation. In 2001, he and his wife, Joyce, founded Shepherd's Tent Ministries, a ministry that supports pastors, ministers, and their wives. This ministry now hosts the Word Conference, one of the premier conferences on the West Coast promoting biblical education and literacy.

He is a graduate of California Baptist University in Riverside, California, and Golden Gate Baptist Theological Seminary in Mill Valley, California.

Pastor Campbell was married to Joyce Elane Campbell for more than forty-nine years before her passing in 2011. He has six children and five grandchildren.

www.ingramcontent.com/pod-product-compliance
Lightning Source LLC
Chambersburg PA
CBHW052148110526
44591CB00012B/1900